FROM TOY

40 years of nursing

By
C.A.Scrimshaw

© copyright 2022 by Carol Anne Scrimshaw

It is not legal to reproduce, duplicate or transmit any part of this document in either electronic means or printed format. Recording of this publication is strictly prohibited.

This book is a memoir. It reflects the author's present recollections of experiences over time. Some names and characteristics have been changed or omitted to protect the identity of individuals, some events have been condensed, and some dialogue has been recreated from memory and may not match the memory of others.

Preface:

Dedications:

Chapter 1:

Persons Of Very Little Importance

Chapter 2:

With Stripes Comes Responsibility

Chapter 3

Three Strikes You're Out.

Chapter 4:

A Bit More Than A Holiday In Blackpool

Chapter 5:

Back Home

Chapter 6

Working On The Bank

Chapter 7

"You'll Be Right"

Chapter 8

Paediatric Conversion

Chapter 9

Moving Up In The World

Chapter 10

New Start

Chapter 11

The Dark Side

Chapter 12

Coming Out Of The Dark

Chapter 13

Cannon Fodder

About The Author:

Preface:

I have wanted to be a nurse since I was 3 years old, well a nurse or a ballerina but as someone born with a dislocated hip way before they tested at birth, dancing would have been too much of a challenge.

Spurred on by Nurse Nancy and the Cherry Aime's girls annual I never wavered from that decision.

I also spent a lot of time in hospital as a child and that had a major impact too.

Due to missing a lot of school with hospital visits and surgeries I struggled academically but as my pre nursing tutor stated in my end of course report "Carol struggles sometimes with the academic side of things but I believe her determination will see her through"

And so here I am at the other side of my nursing career sharing my story with you

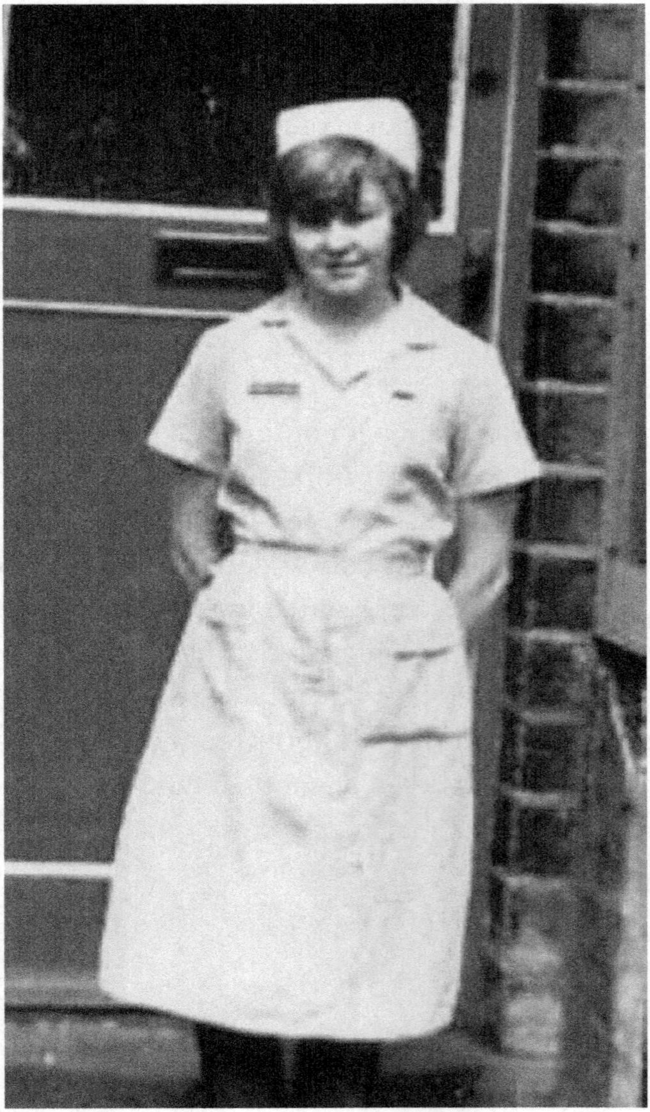

Dedications:

I dedicate this book to all nurses and carers past and present, whether traditional or university trained, we all have a place in the caring profession and we all demand the same recognition and respect for our hard work.

To everyone contained within this book. If you recognize yourself then congratulations! You had an impact on my career whether it is good or bad, it made me who I am today and I thank you for it. Consider that a dedication.

A special dedication to those nurses who are no longer with us: For one of my best friends ever Kerry who I feel will haunt the ward until she gets bored and to Heidi a beautiful soul taken too soon.

Chapter 1:

Persons Of Very Little Importance

It was 9:05 am on January 4th 1981. As I walked up the drive of the Willows, Calderdale School of Nursing I was aware I was late. Feeling so annoyed with myself as I hated to be late. I had even tested the Journey several times and timed it to perfection with time to spare. What I hadn't accounted for was the change in route at different times of day and the fact that the roads had more traffic between 8 and 9 am.

I had left home in Bradford at 07:30, the bus running to Halifax was either the 681 or 682, I must have always caught the 681 on my trial journeys not realising the 682 took a detour around Northowram and the hospital grounds adding twenty minutes on to the Journey. By the time I hit Halifax I had missed the connection up to the hospital. I did not know my way around Halifax well enough to consider walking and it would have taken longer anyway.

As I entered the building, nervous and breathless I was greeted by one of the tutors, "You're late!"

"Yes, I know sorry, I misjudged the buses and missed my connection"

"Connection ? Where have you come from ? "
"Bradford"
"Are you sure? you seem the wrong colour to me, never mind, follow me I will show you where to go" She led me into a classroom and explained the situation, the Tutor at the front introduced herself as Mrs Tyler and told me to take a seat.

As I glanced around quickly, the classroom was set out in rows of single chairs and tables, I guess about 26 student nurses in the class, the only free seat I could see was right at the front, Great! It is an unwritten rule in a class once you are sat in a seat you stay there until the year is over or in this case 3 years.

We began by introducing ourselves, most of the others were local or living in the nurse's home. They all seem to know each other and it kinda left half a dozen of us as 'outsiders'

After the initial introductions we were given our uniforms and given a tour of the building. There was a changing room with lockers and we were advised from now on we would be expected to wear our uniforms at all times. The stiff paper hats were in a neat pile with different variants of stripes, as first year students we were to wear the hat with one blue stripe. We were shown how to fold them and insert a stud in the back to keep it in place. Each day during the first week we would get a new uniform giving us 5 in total.

We had been told to wear black tights and shoes so we were able to change into our uniforms on the very first day. Everyone wore the same black lace up Moccasin style shoes, they were even known as nurses shoes in some shops. I always called them Cornish pasty shoes because of the raised seam around the front. They took some breaking in too as the seam was pretty rough on the inside, once you broke them in though they were like slippers on your feet.

We were also given a cape, navy blue wool with a red lining and red ties that crossed over at the front. The cape was only to be worn when on duty or between hospitals and not to be worn to go home in or in the community. The uniform policy at that time stated you could travel in your uniform but you had to wear a gabardine over it and a navy outdoor hat

Mrs Tyler came to speak to us about the course and asked if we had got the books on the book list. I felt really pleased because I had managed to source them all at the cost of over £100. Most of us raised our hand with a smile." That's a shame" she said "the booklist is so outdated they really need to stop sending it out with the paperwork"

Oh Great!

"On the upside, the next intake will get the same list so if you are fast you can sell them half of it" she said laughing. I still have some of the books if anyone is interested.

The common room was quite spacious and accommodated any students in school. At the time we started there were some second-year pupil nurses there and they had already taken up most of the seats, so we just stood around drinking coffee from the machine and chatting. There was a snack machine too but all main breaks and meals were taken in the hospital canteen over the road.

Walking across the road to the main hospital in my uniform and cape I felt like I was a million dollars, everyone looked so smart and oozing with pride. I had dreamt of this day since I was 3 years old . I had pinned on my brand-new fob watch that mum bought me complete with a glow in the dark second hand, I really looked the part.

We were the last of the nurses that did general nurse training, the following year nurses would be branched out into different specialities after their foundation year, we were also the first nurses who would not get a state badge when we qualified which was disappointing.

The first 6 weeks of the training were made up with; anatomy and physiology, learning basic nursing skills and terminology.

There was a mock-up ward with two hospital beds, we were shown how to do proper hospital corners and making beds with a 'rolling' draw sheet that covered the thick orange rubber bed protector. We were told to have the pillow cases facing away from the door, not just for neatness but to keep draughts from getting inside. Not sure that it helped at all but I still do hospital corners and cringe if pillows are facing the wrong way , even at home !

Initially it was easy for me, bedmaking, taking observations and bed baths as I had done it all while working voluntary on C3 at St Luke's in Bradford. I started there when I was just 15 and I continued to work there on my days off even after I started nurse training. I was very careful not to say so though as no one likes a smart arse.

We were shown how to read a glass thermometer, the last time I had been near glass thermometers was when I had been asked to wash the ones on C3. I collected them all from the back of the beds, they were kept in little glass test tubes fastened to the wall with disinfectant laced cotton wool in the bottom Like an idiot I put them all in hot water, the ends all broke off but I didn't realise until I lifted them out of the water, there were little mercury balls all over the sluice, them little bleeders don't half roll it took me ages to clean up.

Blood pressure was taken manually and you soon learnt how to find a pulse by palpating, everyone was told to draw a little cross on the spot where you could feel a pulse until you perfected it, placing the stethoscope on the cross, the room fell silent as everyone was listening for the change in tone as the sphygmomanometer mercury fell. It was hard at first and you could hear small cheers erupt as each student heard it.

Student nurses were expected to take turns at being the patient for most clinical skills as long as it didn't mean undressing or being too invasive, we had the Resusci-Anne doll for that kind of thing. Having a naso gastric tube passed was one skill we all had to learn and on each other.

"How can you perform it on a patient and reassure them if you don't know what it is like?" we were asked. It is horrible, that is what it is like but not sure I wanted to relay that to any patients. I have to be honest though you certainly have more sympathy when you know what it feels like rather than assuming it is ok. The same goes for blood glucose testing, we did that on the pre nursing course pricking your own thumb with a lancet was scary but not as scary as those who chickened out and were 'stabbed' by the science teacher.

I learnt how to make a kaolin poultice too and it is a bit like algebra I guess because I have never used one nor have, I ever seen one used, I still to this day wonder why it was in the curriculum at all. Probably for the same reason we were given the out-of-date book list !

Lifting technique was an important part of the nurse training, we did not have hoists and it was expected we could manoeuvre the patients safely. My favourite was the Australian lift, although with a dress riding up and a hat in the way it was not the easiest to master. It was probably to blame for the majority of back injuries in nurses.

We were advised of the ward we would be starting on after introductory block and each week we would spend one day on that ward until after the 6 weeks then we would be on placement for 6 weeks.

The timetable was already set for the full three years. 8 weeks on most wards or departments broken up with 1 - 2 weeks in school or annual leave in-between. The wards in the first year were the three primary specialities; medical, surgical and orthopaedic. My first ward was the male medical ward.

Some of the lessons were really boring, like the ones from the pharmacist especially, the guy would come in and talk about drug formulas and my brain would shut off, I just wanted to know the uses and side effects, he did amuse us one time though as he arrived early for the lecture and we were watching a film about varicose vein removal, he passed out at the back of the class and was white and twitching, we thought he was having a fit but apparently you can do that with a simple faint, who knew ? It was hysterical all these new student nurses panicking and yelling for Mrs Tyler to come back.

  The Willows wasn't a typical school of nursing as it was in a detached house, not a college or hospital building. The house had its own gardens at the back that were fenced down the middle half for staff and half for students. We would sit out in the garden for break on nice days and one day someone suggested a game of rounders, the ball kept going over the fence and the tutors got a bit annoyed with us but threw it back anyway.

  The next day we all walked in like we had been hit by a truck, I ached all over, it was a few years since I had played any kind of sport. Mrs Tyler laughed and said we were getting too old and unfit for playing those games and said she had no sympathy for us.

We had several tutors for different classes and one of my Favourites was Mr K, He was quite old and had a thick accent, Polish, I think. He called us "toy nurses" and "people of very little importance" but he had a glint in his eye that made you forgive him. Mr K had a dry sense of humour that I loved.

At that time there were very few male student nurses and when on a female ward they had to be chaperoned, there were three males in our group and each was allocated a female student to be a chaperone. I was paired up with Andy, so for the duration of my training if he was on a female ward I was too, funny how I didn't need a chaperone on a male ward though.

On the second day we went on a visit to the hospital, the Matron was meeting us in the foyer and there were a limited number of chairs, as we all raced to get a chair I felt a thud on the side of my head, one of the girls, Susan, had gone straight into the side of my head with her nose and there was blood everywhere. A passing nurse came over and took her to A and E.

When we got back into school, I was informed she had broken her nose and we should be more careful in future, just a minute she rammed into me! When she came in to nursing school the next day, she had two black eyes and strapping on her nose, I have to admit I did feel pretty guilty, she told me she had to go get her nose fixed in 5 days so I offered to go visit her.

After that Susan and I became pretty good friends, we shared the bus into town but went our separate ways from the bus station. We would bounce different terminology off each other and figured ways to remember it, my favourite word was 'ossification', it is such a smooth word IMO.

Nursing school on the whole was great, we were spoken to like adults and it was nothing like school. I hated school incidentally. All the students had a great sense of humour which is probably a skill necessary to function in this profession.

Holding up a flatus tube Mrs Tyler asked "How would you explain this to a 20 stone lorry driver?"

"I will stick this up your arse and it'll make you fart" I whispered to no one in particular. There was a lot of giggling and I was forced to repeat it to the whole class, it was the wrong answer apparently but she did see the funny side. Sometimes my mouth takes over when my brain has an idea, even saying things that are best left unspoken.

We were taught how to prepare a 2-pint enema with warm soapy water and a funnel, obviously we didn't have to be volunteers for that one !

Each week we were given a test relating to what we had learnt, most of the time the information was fresh in your mind so it was ok. On one of the tests, we were asked to draw a motor neurone and label it, I must have been tired because I misread it as a kidney nephron as I had no clue what the neurone was so assumed it was a typo. We hadn't learnt about the Nephron either but I remembered it from my college days so did a very nice drawing even if I do say so myself.

When the results came back on Monday Mrs Tyler apologised as she had realised, we hadn't done the neurone yet and the wrong paper was given out. I got extra points for my totally irrelevant drawing as I was the only person who even answered the question and she liked my drawing.

It was my first day on the ward, I had to get up at 4:30 to be sure to arrive at 7 am, I was so excited that I hardly slept but I managed to get there early. I always struggle to eat first thing in the morning so hadn't had any breakfast, I sat in handover listening carefully but not understanding half of what was being said, we weren't allowed to take notes so nurses were expected to virtually memorise all 28 patients. The Night nurse sat at the desk with the Kardex reading out each patient one by one; Name, age, consultant, diagnosis and anything that occurred overnight .

All Nurses on the ward were addressed by their surname, no one called anyone by their first name except on break and out of earshot of the patients. As students we were never called by our first names by staff on the ward.

I soon came to realise how intolerant some people can be, as I said, I had the advantage of working voluntary for the last 2 ½ years so knew how things were done, one of the girls who was on the same ward wasn't so lucky, at that time nursing care was based around job allocation and the first thing anyone did after handover was the back round and bed baths.

The ward was a nightingale ward and had 28 beds, the left side was side A and the right ,side B. Myself and the other student were asked to help on side B. As we walked onto the ward following the Aloof staff nurse, the student asked if she should bring the back trolley and the nurse replied "Well it would help dear" in a sarcastic tone and walked off. I was cringing inside.

The trolley was at the end of the ward and had been stocked with bedlinen and towels ready for the shift. I filled the big silver jug with warm water and set it inside the bowl on top of the trolley giving the other student a smile as we followed on.

Most of the patients were already out of bed sat in a chair having breakfast, the smell was making me so hungry, I thought back to my days working on C3 and sister Busfield saving sausages for the nurses and thought it would soon be time for breakfast.

The patients that weren't able to feed themselves were being helped by the auxiliaries and ward orderly, they had bed makers that went from ward to ward so the only beds we had to make were those who could not get up and needed a bed bath and re make the surgical beds when a patient went to theatre.

I asked what time break was and told in a matter-of-fact way that it would be ages yet, the breaks started at 9 am with Staff nurses, then the enrolled nurses and then the students, so allowing for getting to the canteen and back it would probably be nearer 11am! I felt sick and faint by the time I got to go, it was nearly lunchtime! After that first day I made sure I ate before I left home, the only thing I could tolerate so early was a Farley's rusk in milk, if I was late, I ate it dry, smothered it in jam and ate it on the way. Once I got in a good routine, I was there half an hour early so could go to the canteen and have breakfast before my shift started.

Most of the care plans were based on the 'complaint' with very little emphasis on any other problems. Students weren't really responsible for the care plans but we were expected to write in the Kardex. Not the amount you write now though "slept well" was standard on a night shift, writing in black or blue through the day and red at night so it could easily be distinguished when looking for something.

As I said the care was pretty much task oriented so there was a bath book, a dressing book and a folder for the medication charts. Every patient had to have a bed bath or bath at least twice a week and it was documented in the bath book. If they needed any special creams or medications in the bath.

There was a fine art to getting patients in and out of the bath if they could not get in themselves, a stool was placed at the head end of the bath. The patient was sat on the stool and turned around so their feet could be positioned inside the bath. A towel was placed under the armpits from one side to the other to give a better grip and the patient was lifted and slid into the bath. Before they got out you would run the water out, put a towel down their back to aid sliding them out slide them up the back of the bath and back onto the buffet. Generally, it was a two-nurse job but if they were very overweight another nurse would come and lift with a towel under the knees .

The first sign of wholistic patient centred care I came across was based around the 'gingerbread man' we were taught in nursing school. When we had to do a total patient care for an assessment, we started by drawing the shape and labelling the relevant things. Looking at the patient, environment and support network to work out the relevant care. It became second nature after a while. This was my first introduction to the nursing process, I guess.

Essays always started with "The patient was admitted to a warm, well ventilated side room" Ha! like there were that many side rooms available on a nightingale ward.

As much of the necessary care was carried out in the morning because most wards had afternoon visiting. Before visiting started we had to go down the ward and make sure everyone *Looked* comfortable, pillows were plumped, sheets straightened and the bed area was cleared. Each patient was asked if they needed anything. Water jugs were filled up and any rubbish collected. Even the wheels on the beds had to be uniform and facing the right way !

The sister would come to the end of the ward and inspect everything was in order before opening the doors. If she wasn't happy the visitors were late coming in and you would hear them chuntering as they found their respective relatives and friends.

Visiting gave the nurses a little downtime, usually to catch up on the writing of the nursing Kardex. The sister would be in her office and the nurses sat at a table in the centre of the ward, often disturbed by relatives who wanted to ask questions about progress or just to ask for a bedpan or something the patient declined before visiting. The student nurses were encouraged to sit with those who didn't have any visitors and keep them company. The orderly came round with afternoon tea for the patients and those who normally needed help feeding were mostly fed by relatives.

The nurses tea break was taken during visiting time. The afternoon break was only half an hour and you had to get to the canteen in the hospital, they had a system where you could order hot snacks for collection at the time of your break to speed things up. They did things like Jacket potatoes and toasted sandwiches. The canteen was only for staff so the queues weren't that bad either.

I soon learnt that there was a strict hierarchy on the ward, students didn't really speak to the staff nurses, it was customary to talk to the ones on the same level or one up, so as first years we could talk to other students and enrolled nurses if we wanted advice or support. The breaks were divided too, it seemed so strange after my years of working on the ward and feeling comfortable talking to anyone to suddenly finding myself restricted. There was a real knock-on effect if those on top were having a bad day too, ultimately the dark cloud fell on those at the bottom. It wasn't all doom and gloom though; I loved every aspect of patient care and the enrolled nurses were very knowledgeable and eager to support. Some of the enrolled nurses had been qualified for years and had better knowledge than the staff nurses.

Students were expected to give up their seat to a senior nurse and if a sister, Doctor or Matron were on the ward you stood up out of respect.

As nurses we were encouraged to talk to the patients if we had spare time, walk around the ward to see if anyone needed anything, chatting amongst ourselves was frowned upon.

Bedpans and bottles were wheeled into the ward in a heated trolley, after breakfast, after dinner and after tea. The bedpans were stainless steel and often pretty hot when they came out, If the bed pan warmer was not working, they got pretty cold so not sure which was worse. The bottles were made of clear glass and had markings up the side so you could measure the output.

When they had all been used and collected, they had to be taken into the sluice and washed. Students were always allocated the sluice and as it was my first ward, I was lowest in the pecking order so got to do it quite a lot. The bottles were placed over a jet of water to clean them, a bit like the ones they use to clean drinking glasses in a bar. The bedpans had to be emptied and washed out in the big sink and then placed back into the hot cupboard. It wasn't my favourite part of nursing but at least I felt useful.

A common trick the nurses would play on the students is placing a mushed-up Mars Bar in a stool specimen pot or bed pan, they told us that the best way to tell if someone is diabetic wasn't with a urine test it was by tasting the poo. With that the nurse would scoop some up with the little scoop inside and lick it.

" If it tastes sweet, they are diabetic, here you try it"

"Yeeeew, no thanks " I said gipping as the nurse burst out laughing. It wasn't that funny to feel caught out but to the Staff Nurses it was the highlight of getting new students.

Another one was to send you to another ward for a 'long stand', I never got caught out with that one but I witnessed a few students standing at the end of the ward waiting to be asked if they had stood for long enough before being sent back to their own ward. Ha-ha.

When a patient was discharged the bed and locker was washed down with soap and water, the bed was left to air dry before making it up with fresh linen. Another job often undertaken by the students and auxiliaries.

Each clinical skill had to be assessed by the clinical tutors, they would visit the wards regularly to ensure the nurse was settling in and they would come when you felt ready to have a skill assessed. There weren't any assessments on the first ward as it was all about learning the routines and more of an observatory role.

When leaving a ward, I heard it was customary to throw the nurses in the bath in uniform as a farewell gesture. I always made sure I took spare clothes on my last day just in case but they never got me, maybe it is because I lived so far away. Maybe they only did it to nurses who lived in the nurses home. I don't care, I dodged a bullet !

My second placement was on the Orthopaedic ward, that was when I gave my first injection. I wasn't ready! I had practised on an orange and was confident drawing it up but to actually inject a patient was a whole different ball game.

The lady was on traction and bedrest for back pain, I had given her a bed bath assisted by another student nurse and she was complaining of severe pain. I informed the nurse in charge and she said she would give her a painkilling injection. As the nurse headed towards the lady with the little blue tray in her hand she asked if I had given an injection

"No, not yet "I replied

"Today is your lucky day, come on" she said laughing. I was terrified. I rolled the lady onto her side and made the gesture of an invisible cross on her buttock to be sure to avoid the sciatic nerve, Then as I wiped the area the lady let out a blood curdling scream, I damn near shit myself, I looked at the nurse wondering what I had done wrong and she just grinned and said "carry on"

When I actually gave the injection, the lady didn't make a sound, I asked her afterwards why she screamed and she just said it was cold. Apparently, she was renowned for being overdramatic, it would have helped if I was prepared, I won't ever forget my first injection.

I loved the orthopaedic ward; I learned a lot about broken bones and deformities. Everything seemed familiar, things hadn't changed much since my days of being a patient in Woodland's hospital as a child, the traction was the same as it had been for years. Lots of weighted pendulums at the end of the beds. The fractured femurs tended to be the longest staying patients, 6 – 12 weeks on traction and 2 weeks of physio and rehab to get them moving again.

There were a lot of elderly patients, broken hips and joint replacements. I was told that often children who had congenital hip problems needed joint replacements at a much younger age. I was shocked to hear that and even though I did get the odd niggle sometimes when on my feet I didn't want to be looking at a hip replacement at an early age.

Pressure area care was a priority on the orthopaedic ward, two hourly rounds checking for any redness and massaging the buttocks and heels with a mix of alcohol and olive oil, believed to toughen the skin and protect it from friction. I did see some nasty pressure sores, one old lady was admitted with a pressure sore on her sacrum and one on her hip so big you could see through the hole, it was horrific. I doubt the olive oil and alcohol would have prevented that! Pressure areas were often treated with oxygen therapy, basically blowing on the wound with the oxygen tubing on full for half an hour. The wounds were cleaned and packed with gauze soaked in Eusol and liquid paraffin to encourage healing from the inside and each day removed and repeated. This was my first experience of dressing a wound.

    The smell was horrific and there was a machine under the bed regularly pumping out a fragrance equally as obnoxious. These machines were often used with cancer patients too, pretty much like the ones everyone uses in their bathrooms nowadays but ten times bigger and the fragrance wasn't as pleasant.

    There was no way I wanted to do my dressing assessment on a wound like that! When I was ready to be assessed I chose a post operative patient to do my aseptic technique on, for each assessment you had to complete a care plan and look after the patient all day with the clinical tutor coming when the dressing was changed. You didn't wear gloves for dressings so Removing sutures was a real skill using forceps and a no touch technique. The forceps rarely met and had virtually no grip. All the sterile equipment was washed and resterilised in an autoclave machine in the clinic room. The forceps were probably as old as me ! The wards started to use the dressing packs not long after that which incorporated sterile gloves and it made life much easier for any kind of dressing change.

The sisters were in charge of the wards and they all had their own ideas of how things are done, no one ever argued with the sister unless they fancied a relocation. One of the sisters used to put wintergreen on to ease pain in joints and muscles, I am sure she brought it from the stables, it didn't half stink! ha-ha, it wasn't prescribed but at that time many wards had their own little regimes and nothing was banned if it was believed to be in the patient's best interest.

I learnt the importance of passive physio to prevent strictures, some older patients were so curled up it was like the foetal position. Some were that far gone the best you could do was flip them over regularly.

Some patients were nursed on sheepskin rugs to reduce friction although once they had been to the laundry they weren't quite as soft and would leave indents in the skin where the wool had matted together.

As students we were told in school that we were supernumery on the wards, but that information never filtered through to the sisters when you were asked to do a split shift or go help on another ward. I suppose we got a wage so we couldn't complain.

By my third ward, a female surgical ward I was fully aware of the routines and began to relax. With regular pre op injections being given I was fast becoming an expert. Everyone that arrived on the ward was bathed in a Dettol solution and changed into gown and paper knickers before being allowed on the bed. A sign stating nil by mouth was placed at the head of the bed to ensure they weren't offered breakfast.

Pre operative care included shaving in most cases, abdominal surgery patients were given a 'through shave' from above the umbilicus right through to the bottom. It must have been so embarrassing. We just used a Bic disposable razor and talcum powder, I can still feel the grating when I think about it, the only wet shaves were given by a male 'Barber' who would visit the male wards to shave around the delicate genital area with a cut throat razor .

Even if the patient had only been on the bed a few minutes as soon as they went to theatre the bedding was changed to be clean for their return. The bottom of the covers were folded up and the bedding rolled open to one side ready for the patients return. A vomit bowl, tissues and a towel were placed by the bedside, an oxygen cylinder and suction were also brought to the bedside.

The patients were collected and taken to theatre by the theatre staff and brought back to the ward when they had recovered from the anaesthetic.

Observations of heart rate and blood pressure were monitored closely on return. All done manually and documented on the chart.

Most patients were still nil by mouth in the initial post operative period so they had a drip when they returned. I was taught how to count the drips to ensure the right amount of fluid went through at the right rate I had a wooden tongue depressor with all the calculations on it. Everyone was shown how to make one, we covered it in Sellotape so the ink didn't run and you could wipe it clean.

I was asked to sit with a lady who had both her breasts removed, I was told she was only expecting a lumpectomy (although the consent form said to proceed if necessary) and the sister felt she may be a bit upset when she woke up and also, I had to prevent her from lifting her arms up.

I sat by the bed hoping the lady would stay asleep for ages as I was so nervous breaking the news. When she did wake up, she was distraught when she saw the bandages and I had to call the sister to explain.

Surgical patients stayed on the ward until the wound healed, no one was sent home with sutures in and so I got plenty of experience with wound care and aseptic technique. I also got to watch some minor procedures performed on the ward, I watched them open a colostomy once with diathermy, and I fainted, I was so embarrassed. I think it was the combination of the smell of burning flesh and the blood and poo mix that did it.

I was tired most of the time, working five days a week I had to leave home at 5 am for an early shift and didn't get home until 10:30 after a late shift, sometimes I would get to work and the sister would decide I had to do a split shift as there were not enough people on the late shift, this was not optional, they told you the shifts and you did them no matter how hard it was. For a split shift it meant I had to finish at twelve and return at four working through until 9:15pm so not enough time to go home, I would just hang around in between in the canteen and try do some studying, the day was exhausting. After an early shift I would often get home and fall asleep on the sofa, only to be woken up to go to bed at ten and up again the next day at four thirty in the morning.

A few times I was going home on the bus and it went straight past my stop because I fell asleep. I would wake up in the bus station and have to catch another bus home, it was so annoying . One day I fell asleep on the bus, my bag fell off my knee with a bang and it woke me up with a start, I had drool hanging from the corner of my mouth and I felt like crap, there was a little girl stood 3 inches from my face, staring.

" Are you a nurse ?"

" Yes, I am " I said trying to smile, but what I really wanted to say was *'no I am going to a fancy dress party so piss off"*, I am not sure her mum would have been amused.

At the end of the year, we had to take an intermediate exam which was compulsory to pass for me to continue with my training and I failed.

I was finding it really hard to study and work and travel with my homelife a bit of a mess. My stepfather wasn't working and did not allow me to study, most of the time he was disturbing me with the TV on full volume but I couldn't study in my bedroom as it was too cold up there. We didn't have central heating so the living room was the warmest room. One time he threw my books across the room and told me to get off my arse and do some housework if I wasn't working. All the time he was drinking and playing patience with a pack of cards flicking cigarette ash everywhere. My mum was at work but it was common knowledge I didn't get on with my stepfather so it was pointless moaning at mum when she had been working all day.

When I got my results, I was gutted and knew I had to do something. I decided to start doing my studying at the library and so on my days off I pretended I was going to work but instead spent the day at the local library studying and catching up on things I had just skimmed over. I needed to pass this time!

My mum and stepfather had gone away on holiday at the time I was waiting for my results. I had convinced myself I was going to fail again and be thrown off the course, I was so depressed I even contemplated taking an overdose but was afraid of failing that too, what kind of nurse would fail to know what to take to end it all.

I had even lined up every pill in the house I could find. My friend Sylvia called me just in time and that night I ended up going out on a bender instead, it saved my life.

I managed to pass by the skin on my teeth, but hey a pass is a pass!

Chapter 2:

With Stripes Comes Responsibility

As I entered my second year, I was so proud, I got two stripes on my cap and was no longer the junior student nurse. I was expected to help the first-year students and carry my own workload at times.

I found myself back on the medical ward, female this time and on the nightshift. The night nurses would congregate in the corridor of the hospital and then the night sister would call out the names and ward. I was on the medical ward with another student and an Enrolled nurse who was older and very experienced.

The ward at night was very quiet (a word taboo in nursing) and the routine was completely different. We started by giving all the patients who were not nil by mouth an evening drink and the nurse had to wait for the night sister to do the medicine round with her. We collected in all the flowers as I was told they steal the oxygen which I am pretty sure was made up as an excuse so they were not a liability in the dark. False teeth were also collected in pots with the patients name on and taken into the sluice to clean, my biggest fear was dropping the tray and mixing them up but thankfully I never did.

When the night sister came, she would help with the drugs and do a ward round, she would enquire after all the patients as if she really knew them all. I was in Awe; I would have handover and 5 minutes later I would forget everything. Night shifts were good because you had time to read the notes and Kardex properly. One night the sister asked me to do the ward round with her and I was terrified of making a mistake. I thought I was doing well until she asked me why one lady looked yellow

"Maybe she is Chinese? " I said feeling knowledgeable

"No, maybe she has jaundice, you need to learn about your patients nurse!"

Ouch!

The breaks on the night shift were taken individually and you went to the hospital canteen, the most senior going first as always. When the nurse went for her break, we were left on our own, two second years in charge of the ward, there wasn't much happening and everyone was sleeping so it wasn't a problem.

One of the old ladies had been breathing quite noisily and irregular, we were informed it was Cheyne Stokes breathing and not to worry about it unless it stopped, by now we had got used to the sound, but then it stopped, the ward fell silent, I looked at the other student and she looked at me, we walked over to the bedside and we were just staring, willing her to breath. Just as we were about to push the panic button the lady opened her eyes and stared at us, she screamed, we screamed and at that moment the Enrolled nurse came back. I can only imagine what went through her head when she heard the commotion.

When it was my turn for break, I walked up to the hospital canteen, the corridors were eerily quiet and I was starving. I had been told there was a vending machine where you could get hot food and microwave it so I was looking forward to a nice meal. I chose a meal and wondered why it was so dry, I asked why they didn't put gravy on and one of the nurses told me it is in a separate jug on the side and you put it on before heating it, a little late to find that out but I found a cup and went to get the gravy, it was solid, you had to slice it out of the jug but it soon melted in the microwave and it was weak and insipid. After that I started to take my own food to eat, I was not sure how long the gravy was left out or if indeed it really was gravy!

The nightshift week was continuous, one week on and one week off which felt like a holiday on my week off so I loved it. The Enrolled nurse was really knowledgeable and I learnt a lot from her she was so laid back which made it a pleasant environment all round, in fact I found a lot of the night nurses were laid back. The one thing I didn't like were the knitters, I have nothing against knitting but you could guarantee if someone buzzed it would be met with

" It is ok I'll go when I finish this row"

Obviously, that was my cue to go answer the buzzer again, and I heard it so much on a night shift I honestly considered taking up knitting for a break !

I used the quiet time to study or read a book. Being in the middle of the ward we didn't really talk much as it echoed through the whole ward.

During the night we would get some emergency admissions, usually people who took overdoses or intoxicated, it was very rare anything more serious was admitted, they were more likely to go to coronary care or intensive care.

The way the nurse dealt with teenagers that came in drunk was an education in itself. Most were irritable and they were woken every hour to be given a drink and check their neurological status, if they refused or became nasty, she would check the notes to see where they lived and tell them she knew their mum or gran and they often believed her, that was enough to make them behave. I remember thinking when I qualify, I wanted to be like her.

I bought a metro card to travel to work, I would buy it at the end of every month, it had a photocard in one side of a plastic wallet and the bus pass in the other side, each month you would get a new pass stamped with the expiry date.

I was travelling home at the end of February and the bus conductor laughed, he said I would have problems using it the next day as it said 31st February on the date stamp, I said it was only the 28th so what was the problem? I was going to renew it after my week off. He just laughed and wished me good luck. It wasn't until I got home, I realised the next day was the 1st of March and there was never going to be a 31st of February, even on a leap year. I kept it as a souvenir but had to pay on the bus the next day, I was too embarrassed to get it out and did not have time to get a new one, I wish he hadn't said anything because the conductor the next day might never have known.

My next placement was at Northowram hospital, care of the elderly. It was a lovely hospital in its own grounds and took me less time to get to as I caught the bus that went directly into the grounds, on the one occasion I caught the wrong bus I had to walk up the drive, it was like a scene out of Alfred

Hitchcock's The Birds. The trees were full of them and you could tell everyone who had seen the film recently as they were pulling their hoods up and holding them tight around their necks as they ran.

I generally like old people and loved the placement but the ward was overshadowed by some experienced Auxiliaries who thought they owned the place; they would boss the students around and you felt like you had to do what they said to fit in.

In the morning handover we were told if any patients had dressing practice or physio and they were left in bed. I was confused at first so when the auxiliary told me a lady had to be dressed, I got her up and helped her. When the sister came round, she screamed "Who got this lady out of bed?" I told her it was me and she asked if I had listened to handover, I told her I had but the auxiliary told me to get her up,

"And how long have you been taking orders from an auxiliary?" she asked. The sister was in a bad mood all day because it meant this lady had to wait until the next day to have her assessment. I was always careful after that to trust my own instincts or ask a senior before carrying out a task.

They had some weird ideas there too, they mixed ice cream into virtually anything to cool it down or soften it, porridge with ice cream, custard with ice cream, thank goodness they didn't put it on the dinners!

One lady who couldn't speak spat out the porridge every day and when I was asked to feed her, I tried to work out why she wouldn't eat, maybe she just doesn't like it ? I saw she had teeth so gave her cornflakes instead, she loved them, the other nurses couldn't believe I got her to eat, I said it was easy, she doesn't like porridge or sloppy food apparently. I told them I hate porridge and if anyone tries to feed it to me when I am old, they will be wearing it too !

I took my medicine round assessment at Northowram, I had asked for a trial run as I was so nervous so this was a kind of mock exam. It was a total disaster, one of the auxiliaries knew I was nervous so he spent the whole time trying to make me laugh whilst all I wanted to do was concentrate. I know he meant it in good faith but sometimes I needed to be serious to focus on something. The tutor was too busy laughing at him to care.

While the clinical tutor was on the ward the staff nurse in charge asked if she minded keeping her eye on things so she could grab some lunch, there had been only one qualified nurse on shift so it was difficult to go any other time. The clinical tutor said she was happy to so we began the drug round. I was doing so well, checking the name bands and asking the patients for details then we got to one side room and as we entered the lady collapsed.

The tutor shouted for someone to call the crash team and left me stood there, I froze initially as she had the keys in her pocket and I was standing guard of a trolley full of drugs. I closed the lid and pushed the trolley into an empty side room closing the door behind me so I could help with the emergency. By the time I got there it was all over and the poor lady didn't make it. As we left the room the tutor asked where the drug trolley was, I told her I had closed it and put it in a side room out of the way. She was really pleased and said "Well done, I think we can say you passed, I would hate to put you through that again and you acted responsibly even during a crisis"

There were some patients that were so cantankerous and I really did not like them, it bothered me to the point I made an appointment to see Mrs Tyler

"I am not sure I am cut out for nursing after all, there are some of the old people I don't like and I am struggling with my conscience"

Her response was something I carried throughout my career "Are there people in your life your own age that you don't like or you don't get along with?"

"Of course,"

"Well, these people get old, just make sure you are courteous and professional and your personal feelings won't show, try not to worry about it" I never really thought about it like that before but she had a good point.

My community placement was not much of an education, the district nurse I was assigned kept dropping me off for hours at a time at Northowram hospital as she had 'Things to do'. I suspected she was playing away from home; I couldn't prove it but she always seemed much happier when she came to collect me.

She laid down the ground rules:

"Some of these places are insanitary so If I give you my coat don't put it down, If I don't sit down then you don't sit down, try not to pull a face with the smell or look of some places and most of all If they offer you a drink wait until I answer unless you want to get food poisoning" Well, that was reassuring ! For most of the visits I just stood there holding her coat while she did a dressing or gave an injection, I never got to do anything at all.

I had some days out with the health visitor and that was much more fun, we attended the baby clinics and visited new babies at home, I got to give cuddles and gush over these tiny little beings. She was much chattier too so it was a much more enjoyable experience.

I was really looking forward to my obstetric and gynae placement, we had 4 weeks on the gynae ward and 4 weeks on labour/ post-natal ward. For this placement I had Andy working every shift for company too, it was great to have someone I knew on the ward. The women liked it too, he was quite handsome although deep down I suspected he was gay.

I always fancied being a midwife which would mean further training after I qualified so I wanted to make the most of it.

One lady, who had a new baby boy, had a fractured femur and was on traction while I was on the post-natal ward. I got to be stand in mum for all the babies cares, I got to bath him and change him and just hand him to mum for feeds and cuddles. I wanted to keep him he was so cute; it is amazing how attached to a baby you can get after such a short time. (Ironically years later, when I went to have my own baby, the midwife would not let me bath him because there was no one to supervise, I told her about my training and experience but she stuck to her guns, the first thing I did when I got home was give him a bath unsupervised !)

I watched a lot of babies being born and the first time I saw a baby born by caesarean section I cried with the dad in the theatre, it was surreal, one minute I was watching a major surgical operation and the next thing there is a baby crying, WOW!

At the end of the placement, they gave us a 'test' it was so hard it put me off doing my midwifery training, all I could think is if that is a test how hard are the exams? !

The psychiatric ward was a whole different planet. The unit was in a square with a courtyard in the middle. The staff wore their own clothes and addressed everyone by their first names, this was to make it less clinical for the patients. The hard thing was the staff were all crackers and it was hard to tell the staff from the patients. As students we were told we had to still wear full uniform.

It was summertime so we spent a lot of time sunbathing in the courtyard, shoes and tights off, dress pulled up, hair down and no hat, I nearly had a fit when the clinical tutor caught me like that one day, but she didn't bat an eyelid.

We went on a day trip to the seaside with some of the 'stable' patients. They hired a coach and each of us were assigned two patients. They advised us to double up 'just in case'.

One of my ladies went into the toilet, I had to go with her and when she pulled her pants down a wad of money fell out, well over £1000, she begged me not to tell anyone because she was afraid to put it in the bank and felt it was safer there. I had to tell the sister but she wasn't that bothered she just laughed.

An elderly man who had been there because he was suicidal was with my friend, He asked to go in the chemist so we all piled in, He asked for a big box of paracetamol and some razor blades and My friend just let him. I told the chemist he wasn't allowed them and we left, He wasn't happy but laughed at her stupidity.

I never had much of a social life during my training, I lost touch with my school and college friends, many of the girls training with me had a little clique and I was never invited, it was a little far to travel to be fair but it would have been nice to be asked. While I was on my Psych placement, I was invited to a party at the ward sisters house, I didn't really get the option to say no and as the majority of the staff were going, Andy included, I agreed, all I remember was a lot of head banging, a lot of alcohol and sharing a taxi home with one of the girls from the ward. I had been wearing a shirt and tank top (yeah it was the 80's ha-ha) and I got pretty hot so took the tank top off.

The next day I woke up and I had two handbags, I could only think when I grabbed the handle, I took two when getting out of the taxi. I called the ward to tell them and they were just relieved it was found, I was told she would come and collect it after her shift. I was grossly hung over so went back to bed.

The next thing I knew my step father was shouting random shit at me "Why was some strange guy bringing my top home? what kind of prostitute was I? etc. etc."

I got up and Andy was downstairs, he said he had found my tank top down the sofa after I left and brought it back for me. He had tried to leave it but My step father 'demanded an explanation!' and told him to wait, he looked pretty sheepish.

"First of all, this was not a strange guy it was a colleague, secondly I was wearing 2 tops and Thirdly I am 20 years old so you can mind your own business!" I was not in the mood for his bullshit, my head was banging and he had no right to make the poor guy wait anyway.

I thanked Andy and apologised and told him he could go now if he wanted. I was livid!

The topic of the handbag stayed with me for the duration of the placement "Make sure you only have one bag today" or asking everyone if their bag was safely away from mine, they were a great team to work with and crazy as they were, there wasn't a bad bone between them. If I wasn't so scared of half the patients, I could have worked on there

Nurses talk about all kinds of random shit on breaks and one day Andy told me he had never seen a girly mag .The next time I went to visit my cousin in Blackpool I asked her husband if they had any I could have for him. He gave me a couple and put them in a brown paper bag. I felt like I was smuggling drugs back on the coach, I placed the bag on the luggage rack and as the coach took a turn rather fast the bag fell off , the magazines fell out onto the floor. I ended up leaving them where they fell , there was no way I was gonna pick them up when everyone had seen them fall . When I told Andy he said he would have been too embarrassed to read them anyway, hmmm yeah, I was sure he was gay .

CHAPTER 3

THREE STRIKES YOU'RE OUT.

I was nervous about getting my hat with three stripes. In my third year I was expected to take charge, take on a more management role. A third-year student was considered to be senior to an enrolled nurse at that time so we trumped them if there was no sister or staff nurse on shift.

I was on the Gynae ward for night shifts in my third year, the ward was quite small and only had 12 beds. Each night I would set the trolley up "in case of emergency" not having a clue what a real emergency was. I didn't really find that out for many years and with hindsight it was way too much responsibility for a student nurse !

One night when setting up the night sister came to the ward "Are you busy or just trying to look busy nurse ? "She asked. I froze. Night sisters demanded respect, you stood when they entered the ward and only spoke when spoken to.

"I am just setting up the trolley, if you need help with something I can take a break?"

She asked me to do the ward round with her but by now I was confident I knew what was going on so wasn't quite so nervous. When I finished, she praised me and said the following night I was to take charge. Wow! so fast, I only got my 3 stripes a few weeks ago so this was huge. It wasn't an option so I agreed and pretended to be confident.

The next night it was just me and another student, a second year. After the ward round and medicines, we pulled two comfy chairs round to the nurse's desk and got settled for the night. It was very rare for anyone to visit the ward at night so we looked forward to a little relaxation. At about 3 am the Night sisters face just appeared from nowhere, I tried to stand up but my feet were tucked under me on the chair and had gone dead, I collapsed into her arms. I expected to get told off but she just laughed and said we should be a little more alert in future.

My next placement was in paediatrics, I was looking forward to this placement the most.

On the Children's ward there was an outbreak of whooping cough, The sick babies were in cubicles alone and you watched them through the glass, we were only allowed in to give immediate cares and not to comfort or play with them. Parents were only allowed on the ward for visiting an hour a day and there were no overnight stays at that time so there were a lot of crying babies.

Watching the babies choking was one of the most terrifying things I had ever seen, coughing and coughing until they were sick, the little faces full of tears and snot. I swore if I ever had kids, they would be having every vaccination, I never wanted to see anything like that again.

      Entering the cubicle was a task in itself, you put on a gown over your uniform and a mask, the strangest thing was when you took off the gown you hung it inside out on the outside of the door for the next person, they put their arms in the sleeves being careful to only touch the inside of the gown, as we all know bugs don't know how to get from the outside to the inside of a gown , hmmmm. The gown was only changed when soiled or wet. Nurses rarely used gloves then except in theatre and they relied on a good handwashing technique.

      Children that needed regular oxygen were nursed inside an oxygen tent so they could still play, it made sense as toddlers on their own would not tolerate a face mask or nasal cannula like an adult would. We would always have a bed with an oxygen tent made up in case of an emergency admission. When a child went home it would be dismantled and washed with disinfectant solution, you had to be sure it dried properly when put away or it would stick to itself and tear when you tried to use it again.

There was one baby who had a tumour on her face, it was infected and eroding all her cheek and ear. The side of her face not affected was beautiful. The other children would go up to the window and they adored her, such a happy little thing that all the nurses would be scrambling to take care of her.

I got to look after her one day and she was sick, the medication she was on was not pleasant at all, it went down the front of my dress and into my bra. It stunk ! I tried to sponge it out the best I could but the smell was making me feel sick. The sister in charge allowed me to go home early as I didn't have any spare clothes.

I called my mum to tell her I was on my way home and to have a bath waiting for me ! That was the longest bus ride of my career, I sat right at the back because I was conscious of the smell and worried someone might say something.

One day some of the parents made a complaint, they said the other mums had been talking and they did not think it appropriate their kids would be seeing this 'monster' . They had insisted that a curtain be placed in front of the window to protect their children. I was shocked but the sister decided it was easier to comply than listen to them moaning. A screen was placed in front of the window and as soon as visiting finished it was removed. Each day at visiting time a screen was placed in front of the window. Maybe being seen to comply was the secret.

The toddlers had a bay of their own with cots around the outside edges. A blanket was placed in the middle for them to play on with a selection of toys. They all wore terry nappies and potty training was encouraged from as young as 1 year old, younger, if you could catch them quick enough. I loved being in the toddler room, sitting on the blanket playing, it was one of the happier rooms to be in. There were racks of clothes and I loved choosing the outfit for the day, or rather for the next hour until they peed through the nappy or threw up on it. The nappies were rinsed and placed in a bucket of Napisan, once the buckets were full, they were wrung out and sent to the laundry for cleaning.

The older children and those there for surgical procedures were in the long ward. Many were there for their tonsils out, we used to give them 'Aspergum' after the surgery, A chewing gum impregnated with Aspirin for the pain, I loved that stuff! it was great when you had a sore throat, such a shame it got banned. Aspirin was the pain killer of choice for children at that time for the anti-inflammatory properties.

There was a school room at the end of the ward and all school age children went to school during the day, unless they were on bedrest or infectious. It was like a secret club; I never saw inside the schoolroom during my training and often wondered what they did in there, remembering back to my time in hospital as a child and the dragon of a school teacher we had, she even gave me lines for ignoring her when I was asleep !

If children were due medication, I would have to knock on the door to take them out of school and return them afterwards.

The ward would have a strong smell of antiseptic from the 'BIPP' ear packs and nose packs, I hated removing those, they made me gip as much as the patients having them removed, I swear those nose packs were so long they must have gone down to their feet!

My next placement was in Accident and Emergency (A and E) ,we started the day cleaning everything down with a savlon solution. The patient trolleys, the worktops and all the dressing trolleys too the mornings were very quiet and I always arrived early on shift so often I had done most of it before the others arrived.

I was a smoker at the time and a lot of nurses would go in the toilets for a crafty cig during the shift, I never saw a nurse outside smoking in uniform. The sister in A and E was very anti-smoking and one day as I came out sucking a mint, she was coming in.

"Can you believe someone has been smoking in the toilet again? it is like a peasouper fog in there" I said casually as I walked out trying not to laugh. I think she bought it but who knows?

Everyone had polo mints in their packets to try disguise the smell, I realise now, it doesn't work.

I had my ears pierced when I was about 12 but the new fashion was for a double piercing, one of the nurses was getting quite good at piercing ears and she offered to do mine, A bunch of us went down to the minor surgical theatre and she sat me on a chair. "Which one shall I do first?" she asked

"Does it matter?"

"Well, if you chicken out or faint it does ha-ha"

She used the freeze spray to numb my lobe, shit that stuff burns! As she put the huge Cannula through my lobe the sister walked in, I covered my ear with my hand with the needle still in there, my lobe was on fire but I daren't move

"Everything alright girls?" She asked

"Yes, no problem" the nurse said, "we are just having a teaching about the minor surgeries" and the sister smiled and left

"FUCK! that hurts!" I cried.

She removed the needle and used one of my existing studs to put in the hole using the cannula to guide it.

"Ready for the next one?"

I always thought numbing spray was painless so I guess I learnt something that day even if it was just that frostbite burns like a bitch.

Helping in the minor theatre was the highlight of my placement, cutting the sutures for the doctor and watching huge abscesses being popped. On one occasion I was clearing the trolley and when removing the blade from its holder it slipped and sliced across my index finger, the blood poured out. I threw a piece of gauze over it and pressed hard, the blood dripped through my fingers, it would not stop. I shouted for help and no one could stop the bleeding. In the end I had to have it stitched, the other students were encouraged to watch so I put on my bravest face when all I wanted to do was cry. When the doctor realised it was from the nasty pus-filled blade, I had to have a penicillin injection too. They didn't send me home though they made me cover it with a glove until the end of my shift, charming!

Going home one evening there were two boys around 10-year-old, in the bus shelter glue sniffing, I had heard about it but never actually seen anyone doing it. They had little plastic bags and held it over their nose and mouth , they were staggering all over. There were two other nurses there from A and E too and One of the nurses commented on how bad it was for them. One of the boys told her to " Mind her own fucking business" with that she grabbed the boy by his collar and asked me to grab the other. We frog marched them into A and E and insisted they be seen by a doctor; The social services were also called to reunite these little angels with their parents.

I never understood glue sniffing myself, when I was at school everyone hated the stink in the art room.

At the end my placement my report was not very good: Poor for attendance and punctuality, Poor for appearance and the scores out of ten throughout were in the middle all the way. I was really disappointed but the sister who gave me the report more or less said sign here, no feedback and to be honest I hadn't worked with her much at all.

When I went back into college Mrs Tyler called me to her office to ask what went wrong

"I don't know, I felt I did well so couldn't understand it"

"So why did you sign it?"

"I thought I had to?"

"No, you never sign to something you don't agree with, you realise this goes in your file and does not look good for you after you qualify?"

"Well, what was I supposed to do?"

"Did you agree with it at the time?"

"No"

"So, WHY DID YOU SIGN IT?"

"I don't know" I felt broken

Mrs Tyler asked what I did not agree with and said she would go back to the sister asking her to change it.

I told her I was early every day; I was never late, not ever since my first day in nursing school. I wore my uniform correctly, my hair was always in a bun, I never wore makeup and my shoes were always polished so could not understand why that was seen as poor, after that the rest is opinionated, I did not see how anyone who never worked with me could have an opinion of me.

"Leave it with me, I will see what I can do" "OH, and Carol, don't ever sign anything you don't agree with "she said as I left the office.

I was always careful signing reports after that.

My placement in the operating theatres was not enjoyable at all despite my mum telling everyone I wanted to be a theatre sister (I have no idea where she got that from but I never corrected her lol). The first two weeks all I saw were cystoscopies. It was so boring, even when you got to help it was a matter of standing on a step and pouring water into a glass bottle, keeping it topped up throughout the procedure, then watching it pour out into a bucket on the floor. The doctors never told you what you were seeing on the screen so they could have been watching a cowboy film for all I knew.

The staff were horrible too, sarcastic and very much a clique. Most of the time they would send a bunch of students to the linen cupboard to 'study' basically we sat around bitching about the bitching so we learnt nothing.

One of the students from my group had been watching an orthopaedic surgeon perform a hip replacement, as they cut the end of the femur off it rolled on the floor, she had been assigned the swab rack, basically picking up swabs with big clamps and hanging them on a rack for counting, when she saw the bone fly, she went to pick it up off the floor carefully with the clamps and threw it right in the middle of the sterile field. The surgeon virtually threw the tray at her and screamed for her to be removed from the theatre, she left after that.

    When we got our reports, they were very poor. I knew from experience not to admit to the lies and refused to sign it, the other girls did the same. The matron was called and we said we had learnt nothing and the reports were not a true reflection of our time there as no one had wanted us around from the start.

    The Matron asked if the sister changed the marks would we sign it but we said that was not the point, in the end she told us we had to sign it and if we disagreed to make a comment at the bottom. I wrote "This report does not reflect my placement here, I did not learn anything and It would have been more beneficial if the attitude of the staff had been better", then signed it. The other girls all wrote something similar.

    The Matron and sister weren't happy but when it got back to the college of nursing, they decided it would be better to have a better presence of the clinical tutor during that placement so that things could be addressed early on instead of when it was too late.

I found myself back on my very first ward for my final placement, the sister was so nice and was so supportive. I loved it on there.

The hospital exam went well and I passed first time, I was so relieved as the work /study balance had not really improved much over the three years.

Unfortunately, I did not do so well in my state finals, I was devastated! I passed the multi choice exam but the main paper I had not got a good enough grade. The only option was to resit. In between I was allowed to stay on the ward as a student. The sister was just as disappointed as me, she had wanted me to qualify and get a job on her ward.

I had gone to the canteen and a nurse who had joined our group in the final year came and sat at my table

"I hear you failed" she said with a grin

"Yeah, so why do you feel the need to be so nasty?"

She just laughed and walked off, I never liked her anyway

Not long after that we found out she had been found dead in her new house she had just bought , she was due to get married soon too, I never got any details or information but we were all questioned by the police.

"Do you know anyone who might want her dead?"

"Quite a lot I imagine she was not a nice person at all"

I never saw anything on the news or heard anything about it after that, sad really, she had everything going for her and it was gone overnight.

After failing a second time I was given the option to take the enrolled nurse exam or have one final attempt. You were only allowed three attempts at the exam and after that you had to take a break of 5 years before restarting, I had 3 years to resit the exam, if I failed, I couldn't even do the enrolled nurse exam.

The situation at home had not improved and so felt it was in my best interest to take the enrolled nurse exam then, leaving me another attempt within 3 years if I felt I wanted to.

I passed the enrolled nurse exam first time, maybe because it was multi choice, (I read somewhere a monkey could pass a multi choice just by randomly touching boxes) Instead of being happy and looking for a job I just wanted to get out of Calderdale away from the other nurses who had passed, they were all now working as Staff nurses on the wards, in effect as I passed my exam, I became Junior to myself and that was not what I wanted.

Mum bought me a beautiful ornate silver buckle when I qualified, getting your buckle and belt was a rite of passage for nurses and felt really special. I loved it but felt disappointed taking it to the sewing room to have a green petersham belt attached. I had been so looking forward to the purple one.

Chapter 4:

A Bit More Than A Holiday In Blackpool

There were no jobs advertised in Bradford and I spent a short time working behind a bar while I decided what to do with myself. The pub was managed by my cousin Kath and her husband Dennis, the job wasn't Ideal but it got me out of the house and gave me more money than I got during my training so I stuck it out. I had a row with Dennis after a shift one night over something pretty trivial and quit, with no other prospect I needed time to sort out what I wanted to do with my life. I didn't spend all that time training to work behind a bar.

When I got really fed up, I would often go and spend some time at my cousin Sue's guest house in Blackpool. I gave Sue a call on the Thursday night and arranged to go the next morning for the weekend. It was always cheaper to get a day trip ticket and just not go back, I would just go to the bus station in Blackpool and buy another day ticket when I was ready to go home, only using the return portion.

When I arrived at the guest house Sue was just about to go for her morning walk around the block to do her shopping so I tagged along. When we passed the job centre Sue suggested I go see if there was anything in Blackpool, she said I could keep my room as long as I needed and so I went in.

The Job centre was pretty much the same set up as the one I had been in at Bradford; the central area was filled with people sat at desks and there were racks of cards all around the wall with all kinds of Jobs. I found one for a local Nursing home and took it to the next available advisor. The guy called the nursing home and arranged an interview the same day, I didn't have a CV or any kind of ID with me but that didn't seem to matter.

That afternoon I went for an interview for a night nurse job in the nursing home, it seemed to go well and I went back to Sue's. That same day my brother Dennis and his girlfriend Angela arrived from Bradford for the weekend, a spur of the moment thing so we didn't know they would be there. My brother said he would give me a lift home on Sunday if I wanted to save me going back on the coach and I said I would wait to see if I got the Job first.

On Sunday afternoon I still hadn't heard anything about the job so I phoned them, I explained I needed to know as I would be travelling back to Bradford if I hadn't got the job.

"OH NO! Didn't anyone call you? We are expecting you to start for an orientation shift tomorrow, Matron was supposed to call before she went home on Friday" The nurse went on to say I had been put down for the night shift on Tuesday and Wednesday of that week after my orientation day, and I would be working a rota of Monday to Wednesday one week and Monday to Thursday the next. I was asked to go in at 9 am on the Monday morning.

I was stunned, I had never started a job that fast before and I didn't have anything with me, not even spare knickers to get me through the week, no suitable shoes or tights or anything, I didn't even take any spare cash. Angela told me she would leave her credit card and I could pay her back when I got paid, phew! Luckily in Blackpool the shops are open late so I could go buy some clothes and shoes. Sue told me the room was mine as long as I needed it.

The nursing home was a short walk away from the guest house, I could even walk along the prom with a minor detour. The Matron was there to greet me and apologised for the mix up. I reassured her I was just happy to get the job so it was only a minor hitch.

I was still a little concerned that she had not asked to see my ID or certificates. I had given her my registration number and a phone number of The Willows to Check for a reference, The matron said she had checked it against the register and spoken to my tutor and was happy I was who I said I was. She told me she would photocopy the other things when I could get back to Bradford to collect them.

I was given a pink uniform, pink? I had never seen a pink nurse's uniform before but I was told it had been sent in error and my uniform would be lilac when it arrived.

My job role was outlined and told unfortunately there would not be anyone to show me the ropes but Judy had been there a long time so she would let me know the routine.

The nursing home had 50 beds but the patients were mostly mobile and so the workload wasn't as big as it seems for one nurse and one carer on a night shift. The Matron was always on call for back up if needed.

There was a real friendly atmosphere in the home, the nurses and carers all worked well as a team and I felt I would be happy there. One of the nurses commented I would be working with Judy the witch and I was a tad nervous to be honest, apparently no one liked to work the nightshift with her as she was a little creepy and the last nurse had left suddenly, Great!

The first nightshift It was just me and Judy, she didn't seem at all creepy to me in fact I thought she was really nice. She was a little older than me but could not do enough to help, the patients loved her.

I was responsible for the medications and Judy was responsible for suppers and putting the patients to bed. Once I had finished my drug round, I helped Judy with those who were heavier and she needed help with.

We had a list of jobs for the night shift but Judy did most of them, cleaning the chairs in the lounge, unpacking the linen sacks from the laundry, rinsing the dirty bedding and bagging it up ready for collection and we even had to prepare the vegetables for the next day so each night we filled a bucket with peeled potatoes in varying shapes for chips or mash etc.

We were sometimes left a meal from the day caterer or we were allowed to make sandwiches and snacks from the kitchen at night.

I would eat a dinner before I went to work, sometimes a 3-course dinner (Bonus of living in a guest house) so I only really snacked at night, if I was hungry in the morning, I would call Sue to order a cooked breakfast before bed. Judy didn't believe I was eating and called Sue once, she said she was afraid I didn't eat enough and ate like a bird, Sue said "yes, a hawk!"

We both walked around the bedrooms every two hours to check all was well, changing positions, bedding and pads as required, the patients all had a buzzer so they could call for help if they needed to, most of them had sleeping tablets so to be honest it was rare for anyone to wake or need anything.

We did have a couple of wanderers and the fire door alarm didn't work so it was important to do regular checks, luckily, I had no escapees when I worked there. One guy kept buzzing all night but when I went in, he pretended to be asleep and the buzzer was on the floor, I was getting really frustrated and when I told Judy she said he was notorious for pleasuring himself and the vibration made the buzzer fall on the floor, she told me to tie it on the bedstead next time, amazing what little tips you can pick up ha-ha

When we sat down for a rest and our first cuppa of the evening it gave us chance to get to know each other, after all I would be working exclusively with Judy 3 or 4 times a week so it was important, we got along.

Judy asked me who Leonard was, at first, I thought she was referring to a patient and my biggest fear is we had a runner, I said I didn't know there was anyone called Leonard, she said "No, not a patient, he said he is your dad"

    What? My dad was called Leonard but he died when I was six, how did she know that? Judy could see I was confused and told me not to worry she had a gift and people of the past came to her a lot. She told me my dad had been hounding her for weeks about me and she had no clue who he was talking about until I started. So not only had she been 'talking' to my dad, she knew I was coming even before I applied, this was just getting weirder. I was starting to understand what the other nurses were warning me about but it was the middle of the night and I was kinda obligated to stay.

    Judy told me my dad just wanted to let me know he was still watching out for me and had told her she better be nice so I guess it wasn't that scary after all, whether I believed her or not was another thing. The only person I knew in Blackpool was Sue and so I cannot find any other possible way she would know that information, she even told me my dog Mitzi (a dog we had as kids) was sat by my feet all the time.

    Maybe that's why I am always tripping over nothing and it isn't just because I am gormless

    I did ask Judy if she had these powers why wasn't she on the prom with the other clairvoyants instead of working in a nursing home, she said it was a 'God-given power' and if she abused it, she would lose it. She also told me anyone who charges money is a fake as they would lose the gift if using it for personal gain. She told me they are always vague and never specific, I bet one of those wouldn't have pulled my dad's name from nowhere! Made me think anyway.

Judy also practiced Yoga, she would sit in the middle of the floor cross legged humming, she never noticed me laughing so she must have been in the zone.

As the shift went on things got back to normal and I really liked Judy, I decided to accept her 'quirks' and not to let it worry me. We made a great team; she was always finished in time on a morning to make a bacon sandwich and cuppa before the day shift arrived.

At handover some of the day staff had been concerned about one gentleman When they asked how he was this morning I said he was 'hard on' In Bradford that means asleep, apparently not in Blackpool and I shocked everyone "You can't say that! " OOPS!

At the weekend I managed to go home to Bradford and brought some things from home, I collected my nursing badges, certificates and most important of all. my belt buckle. I unpicked the green belt and threw it in the trash. I bought some white petersham and sewed that on instead. My Lilac uniforms had arrived so the white belt looked great.

Sue's husband Howard was ill, he had seen a lot of doctors but no one seemed to get to the bottom of it, he was unable to swallow and lost a lot of weight, he was in constant pain too. I had been talking to Judy about it and she asked me to bring something of his in and she could help.

I took one of his handkerchiefs in and she held it in her hands for a while, when she gave it back it was red hot, Judy said to keep that with him and it would give him a little relief but she could only see blue, when I asked what that meant she said she couldn't say any more than he would be at peace. WTF?

With no doctors wanting to help they went private and found out he had cancer. Howard had always been like the dad I needed and I was really depressed after that.

I loved my job, I loved living in Blackpool and Sue and Howard were great too, my rent was minimal and in return I agreed to help in the guest house and run the bar on the Thursday nights on the alternate weeks I was off work.

The only problem was I was homesick, I never wanted to go back but I missed my mum like crazy, she was my best friend, I didn't really have that many friends at home to be honest, everyone from school and college went their separate ways for work/ study and made new friends.

I never really got to know anyone while living in Blackpool as there was just the two of us on shift and I never got to know any of the day girls, I handed over and went home in the mornings. I was always fascinated with the tan the girls had and when I asked, they said they used Bryll Cream "The oil and lemon juice give you a good tan" they said. I did buy some but never used it because I never really knew if they were joking. I had visions of me going into work with a face like Rudolph's nose

Judy was married and older and so I never saw her out of work. On my birthday I invited her over for a drink to celebrate and Sue baked me a cake, Judy came but she seemed anxious to leave, she told me she had brought me a card and gift but couldn't stay long as her husband was waiting outside in the car. Her husband kept papping the horn and shouting at her to hurry up but when she went outside, he just sped off.

Judy seemed terrified and started crying, Howard offered to take her home and I never saw her again. On my next shift I was told she wasn't working there any longer but I never found out why, I tried to call her and her husband answered the phone, he was really nasty and told me not to call again. I guess her 'gift' didn't extend to recognising a narcissistic control freak. I was sad but I had to accept that I was never going to see her again. I didn't even know where she lived as she had insisted Howard leave her at the end of the street.

I was introduced to Betty my new colleague on my next shift ; she was young and a joy to be around. We hit it off instantly. The work routine was just the same as with Judy but Betty was funny and we chatted for hours. We would watch TV in the lounge until the red dot and then listen to the radio in between the checks.

Betty loved to listen to the chat show on Red Rose radio, The guy was notorious for hanging up on people if he didn't like their opinion but Betty called in a few times and kept him going for ages. I would listen in the lounge laughing.

On our nights off we would hang out together, shopping in the day and clubbing at night, it was great fun having drinks bought by all the eager holiday makers to leave them hanging at the end of the night. Drinking our way through the cocktail menu and then I would tell them I lived with my Auntie and she was strict so I had to go and we would go back laughing.

One night shift we were doing the rounds and when we got back in the lounge two police officers were sat there

"You really need to be more careful leaving windows open; anyone can get in "one said laughing.

"As seen as we are here, any chance of a cuppa? "

"Yeah, on one condition" Betty said, "You go get us a donor kebab"

They both laughed and said they would. The kebab shop was only a street away and they came and joined us for supper. The police officers came regularly for break after that but entered through the door not the window.

The windows at the front of the nursing home were tinted glass so we could see out but they couldn't see us unless the main light was on, we would just have a little light on at night, it was a double front with an inset porch that was directly onto the pavement. We often got entertained by young couples standing in the doorway snogging or arguing not realising they were being watched, some guys even used it as a urinal but ended up pissing on their shoes when Betty opened the window suddenly calling them a Dirty B*stard.

By now I had brought most of my clothes and important stuff to Blackpool . It was getting a little chilly and one day when I went to put on a Jacket, I found more than £200 in the pocket. I was happy but puzzled at first then I remembered, before I came to Blackpool I had just been paid.

My Friend Sylvia had her purse pinched once at a night club and lost all her money, after that whenever I went out, I would take the exact amount I needed and put the other safe in a pocket or different bag. When I originally went to Blackpool, I just took what I needed for the weekend .U2sing Angela's credit card to pay for things and then being paid while I was there, I totally forgot about the money in my Jacket, what a bonus !

There were a 100-year-old brother and sister admitted while I was there, they were twins and never been apart their whole life so it was agreed they could share a double room with a screen between them at night, seemed a bit creepy to me but it was not my decision. The lady had never washed her hair for over 60 years, she was a believer that the natural oils in your hair kept it clean once you got out of the daily wash cycle, one of the day nurses had given her a bath and washed her hair, she said it was minging but got into trouble all the same.

The home was a firm believer in keeping everyone's routine as near to home as possible which I thought was great until this brother and sister insisted on a soft-boiled egg and soldiers at 6 am every morning, right in the middle of the rounds so it messed up our routine completely. The caterers didn't arrive until 8 to make breakfast and apart from the odd slice of toast we were not responsible for serving breakfasts at all. We did make a big pan of porridge every night ready for the morning so I suggested they have porridge instead but they refused.

The Matron was great with the staff and patients, she was so supportive, at the weekend she would pick up some of the old dears and take them to her house for afternoon tea, not just the mobile easy ones either, she would take the cantankerous ones and those who needed a wheelchair. She rotated between the patients giving them all a turn.

Sometimes when I was walking around the local markets, I would see staff taking the patients shopping or to the beach too. It must have been a lovely place for them to stay.

When Judy or Betty was on holiday, I worked with a nurse called Clair, she normally worked the weekends but did the shifts as overtime to cover holidays etc. Clair was a friend of the Matrons but I didn't like her. She wanted to take charge and I more or less took the role of the Carer, anything for a quiet life. Not many people liked her she was very dominating and although she acted like a know it all there was something about her that didn't sit right with me. A lot of the patients told me she was smacking them and not nice at all, they hated it when she was on shift. I had no reason to disbelieve the patients so couldn't just ignore it.

      When I mentioned it to the Matron, she said I wasn't the first to tell her and she was getting concerned. She told me her credentials seemed to be in order and without proof there wasn't a lot she could do.

      When I went in for my next shift, I was informed Clair had been arrested. I was told the nursing registration number she was using actually belonged to her mother, they both had the same name but her mother had died ten years previously. Seems she was a bit of an opportunist and never even trained as a nurse at all! This hadn't been her first nursing job either which is how she had known the matron from a previous post. I guess working with someone in a role you would easily assume they were qualified, I did think how easy it was for me to start there though without a shred of evidence. All I could think of was how I left her to give out the medications while I changed the shitty nappies! She even had the neck to ask me to make her a bacon sandwich in the morning!

Howard's health was deteriorating and Sue made the decision to go be near her family in Bradford, that meant selling the business so I needed to find somewhere else to live. The next-door neighbour offered me a flat he was in the process of renovating. I gave it a lot of thought and as much as I loved Betty, she had a boyfriend at home and I was alone there, I decided to move back to Bradford too. Betty wasn't happy but we promised to keep in touch.

I really didn't want to go back home as long as my stepfather was around so I was looking for accommodation of my own, Angela and Dennis had broken up but Angela was still a close friend and she offered me a room at her house to rent. Mum had been so excited about me coming home she had rung around nursing homes in Bradford telling them some sob story and got me an interview at one the day after I returned.

Chapter 5:

Back Home

I moved in with Angela and we settled in pretty easily, I got the job at the nursing home and started the following week. I knew right away this nursing home was not of the same quality as the one in Blackpool

As the manager showed me round, she introduced the patients as private or DSS. I asked her why and she said "surely you understand those who are paying deserve a better quality of care?"

"But even the DSS patients deserve the best of care, someone is paying for the care even if it isn't them"

I am not sure she was impressed with my response but to be honest if she had sacked me at that point I wouldn't have cared.

None of the rooms had en suite just a bed and, a chair and a cabinet. Some had their own TVs brought in from home

The private rooms were all single and DSS rooms were double rooms,

The Matron there did not have a presence at all, she was living in and was on call only. There were lots of care assistants but they were all very young and many were inexperienced. A qualified nurse was assigned to each shift so in the afternoon there was a bit of an overlap otherwise it was one nurse and numerous carers.

The home had a strict regime of toileting and bedtimes, The night staff got everyone up from 6 am and sat them in the day room, they went for breakfast in the adjacent dining room, after meals they were all taken to the toilet and then back in the day room, virtually everyone who could not mobilise themselves wore a nappy pad in between meals. a solitary TV was at one end of the day room.

I never saw any activities and visitors were scarce, usually when visitors were expected the patient was returned to their room for 'privacy'. It was far too regimented and the patients didn't seem happy at all.

The day room was a square with chairs around the edge, the secretary's office was attached to the day room so she insisted no noisy patients were in there during the day. Many times, she would come and ask for one removing back to bed as they were annoying her.

At 3 pm we started putting the patients back to bed or in the chair in their room, they had their evening meal in bed. I had never seen a routine so rigid since working on the elderly ward at

Northowram, but this was supposed to be their home, I was shocked.

The handyman had a room there after a break up from his marriage and we got talking, he was fun to be around and made the job much better, after a few weeks we started dating.

when the Manager found out we were in a relationship she started being really nasty towards me, some of the girls said she had designs on him but to be honest she was older and fatter and obviously delusional.

The first time I had sex I got pregnant, it was one of those things that happened to other people not me ! The manager got wind I was pregnant and made my job very difficult, someone said she would try get rid of me because she hated paying maternity pay. She was insisting I lift heavy patients with inexperienced carers and skip breaks; I hated it there.

I had a miscarriage on Valentine's Day, we had already decided to get married and so my boyfriend booked the wedding for June of that year. Things got even worse after we got married

There had been a staff meeting in the middle of my night shifts so I hadn't been able to attend, the first news I got was on my day shift and it turns out they had stopped providing lunches for the staff, without a canteen there was no alternative but to bring a packed lunch, I didn't find out until I was on shift.

It had been a particularly stressful shift due to staff shortages and lack of experienced staff, I was sent for lunch one hour before I was due to go off shift, when I went into the kitchen I was told about the change of plan, with no food available I offered to go without a break and leave earlier, the manager said that was out of the question and I should take my break now, I was tired and hungry.

"If you had been to the staff meeting you would have known about the changes" she said in a smug tone

"How could I? you had it right in the middle of my night shifts, you could have told me when I came in last week instead of waiting until It was time for my break" I was fuming.

"You cannot expect me to work all day without food "I shouted "there is nowhere to get food from and I could just go half an hour later and go straight home"

"You don't know what work is" she screamed in my face "If you want to keep your job here you will do as you are told"

"STICK YOUR JOB UP YOUR ARSE! "I shouted over my shoulder as I walked out the door.

It could have been hunger talking or a hormone thing as I had also just found out I was pregnant again. I tried to sign on but I was told I couldn't get paid for six weeks because I had left of my own accord. If I had been sacked that would be a different matter. I doubted anyone would employ someone who was pregnant so was pretty annoyed with myself. Looks like I was 6 weeks without any money.

The next morning, I got a letter through the post telling me that as I had left the premises without permission I was fired, I contacted the dole office and was told if I brought the letter in, I would get paid straight away. I wonder if the stupid cow knew she had just done me a favour !

My husband seemed supportive and he said she was making it difficult for him too but he stuck it out. The following Sunday he got a call to sort out a problem at the nursing home He figured he could call in on our way to visit his mother. I sat outside in the car while he went in to sort things out, ten minutes later he came out and said some of the patients and staff were asking to see me so I went inside to visit them.

On Monday morning I got a phone call from the manager

"I hear you were here yesterday, Is that true?"

"Yes, I visited a couple of the ladies at their request, I had been waiting outside for my husband at the time"

"You are not welcome on the premises and if I hear you have been again, I will call the police!"

"Yeah whatever" I said and put down the phone

When my husband found out he was fuming and called her, he said he was asked to bring me in by the patients and I had as much right to visit people as anyone else. In the end he said he quit too and put down the phone. He reassured me he could work for himself and not to worry

I worked briefly in another nursing home on nights but I didn't like it there at all. I would get paid for my breaks as 'on call' but the two carers on shift didn't. One night one of the carers asked if I fancied KFC and I said yes why not, the other carer declined.

The next day I was in bed and I got a call from the nursing home asking me to go straight in as a matter of urgency. I got a taxi as it seemed like a life-or-death situation. When I got there the manager said she had been informed that I allowed the carer to leave the premises to go for take away the night before. I said yes, the home was all settled and she was on her break.

I was told she should not have gone out as it was dangerous to leave just the two of us and she had no alternative but to sack her. She told me to consider it a slap on the wrist

"What? you sacked her for taking a break that she wasn't paid for?"

"Yes, because she left the building"

"But surely if she isn't paid for her break she could go home if she wanted?"

"No, it isn't safe"

"So, who told you about it anyway? The other carer?"

"Yes, she was concerned and stayed behind this morning"

"Tell you what, I don't want to work with a jealous grass, if the other girl is sacked because I allowed her to go out then I should leave too"

I was sick of the whole 'caring' profession by now so once again I was pregnant and unemployed.

When I was 3 months pregnant with my son My husband got sent to prison for Arson, he had set fire to someone's bike because he had owed him money and blew half the house away the night before we got married, I knew nothing about it until the police came hammering on the door three months later. He was still in prison until my son was 6 weeks old. When he came home, he promised everything would be great, he would work for himself and I needn't go to work at all we would manage.

I didn't really work much for the next few years until my son Daniel was about 3 years old. I worked the odd bank shift at the library but no nursing jobs as I was sick of being abused as an enrolled nurse and decided I had just one last chance to resit my exam to be a staff nurse.

I applied to resit my exam and it was arranged for me to take it in Bradford school of nursing. I spent the next few weeks studying hard, I was determined to pass this time and I did.

When I got my final results, I was contacted by Calderdale school of nursing, they told me when I qualified as an Enrolled nurse, they had given me the hospital badge and certificate for an Enrolled nurse even though I had passed the hospital exam for a Registered nurse.

Obviously at the time I could not be given the hospital badge and certificate for a registered nurse after failing my finals. The UKCC had contacted them so they could amend their records and they gave me and appointment to collect the badge and certificate. They said I was joining the group that had just qualified so they had put on a little party, they told me I could bring someone with me too.

My mum came with me and when I got there it turned out to be a full award ceremony and mum was so proud, I thought she would burst.

My first job as a Staff Nurse was at a private medical slimming clinic. I was responsible for weighing the clients, taking observations, giving out prescribed medication and documentation. It was better paid than the enrolled nurse jobs and I was in charge of my own workload.

I worked just two days a week which were the two days my husband didn't work. It was hard because half the time I would go home to find he had dumped Daniel at his mother's and gone fishing or gone out for the evening. I would have to go to his mothers on the bus to pick him up as it was before mobile phones and I had no idea when he would be home if at all. We certainly didn't have money for taxis. His mother had a car but she never used t to help me out. Even later when her son was in Killingbeck hospital in intensive care after having heart surgery, she told me to get the bus with 3 kids!

The manager from the nursing home came in one day

"Fancy seeing you here" she said looking embarrassed.

"Yeah, you are on my territory now" I replied with a grin as she stepped on the scales.

It was customary to write down the weight and show the clients the card discreetly, but I took great pleasure in shouting out her weight to her in the waiting area. Oddly enough she never came back. Pity really because she really needed to lose weight. Some of the clients really didn't need to be there, girls of 8 stone nothing on a "maintenance programme"

The clients were given appetite suppressants and had a meeting with the doctor and the coach / dietician each visit. They had to keep a food diary too. The philosophy of the clinic was no food is bad and you can eat whatever you want and lose weight.

The secret? It isn't really rocket science, it is all about the amount you eat, yes you can eat cake but only a 1" square. The 'Coaches' were barely trained and just told the clients to eat minimal amounts of everything. A salad was basically one slice of everything, eat on a side plate and those that needed to lose weight would benefit from this advice, taking the appetite suppressants was the key to it all.

Everyone lost weight in the first week as they were given water tablets as well as the appetite suppressants to give them the boost they needed to kick off. They were told to take those on the morning of their next appointment.

Those on the maintenance programme paid £33 a month just to be weighed and get a pat on the back!

The Doctor who owned and ran the clinic had other clinics too, I worked in the other clinics sometimes; The doctor would take me in the car to the Leeds clinic. Virtually all the staff there smoked and she was very anti-smoking. She knew I smoked but did not know all the others did. I used to go out the back and never got caught. One day she came and said she could smell smoke in the office. I knew who it was but she blamed me as she thought I was the only one, I told her I go out the back, if she comes in, I walk around the front and she would never catch me. I told her she needs to look closer at the other staff.

The Doctor's no smoking policy even extended to works parties, it was banned so I never went. She offered me her cast off clothes as I was as skinny as her but it was all designer wear and I would have no use for clothes like that. I rarely went anywhere and at work I wore a uniform. With hindsight I should have said yes and sold them.

I was 7 stone wet through at the time and never gained weight no matter what I ate. She advised me to eat ice cream after every meal if I wanted to gain weight but, in all honesty, I think it was good for the business if I stayed thin.

The owner would see people for their initial assessment but the doctors doing the prescribing at the clinic were all retired or GP's earning a little extra cash, they would talk to the clients about the medical side of things. As long as their observations were within normal limits and normal body functions were happening there was very little to say.

One day I was called into the office, the accountants had been concerned about my pay, apparently, I was earning more than the coaches and she wanted to ask if I would take a pay cut or reduce my hours by taking a longer break. I told her I wasn't prepared to take a pay cut as I felt it was average for my level of qualification and the reason it was more than the coaches is because they only had in house training which was not on an even par to my qualifications.

    For a while I extended my lunchbreak but the day was just as long and I got less money .At first, I would go in a spare office and read a book while I had my lunch, the staff there weren't allowed hot or strong-smelling food in case the clients could smell it so it was usually a boring ham or cheese sandwich The other staff would come in asking me to dispense tablets or do a quick weight 'because I was there anyway'. It got frustrating that she insisted I have a longer break with no pay yet utilised me during that time.

    On a nice day I would go to the park until a policeman told me it was not a good idea to be in a nurse's uniform, in the park ,on my own in Manningham, because people would think I am in a whole different profession. Charming !

    I started to go to Manningham Library where my sister worked as I knew everyone there from my bank shifts. I was allowed to go in their staff room which was much better than sitting in a poky office on my own. It also meant I could have hot food, fish and chips or pie and peas from the local shops.

I started to think maybe I was paid too much so had a look in the job centre. I then realised I could be getting a lot more working on the nurse bank than I got at the clinic, the pay I was on was not much more than what I got as an enrolled nurse and a staff nurse pay was a lot more.

I gave in my notice and started looking seriously for other work.

Chapter 6

Working On The Bank

I started on the bank at Bradford Royal Infirmary working on the Paediatric ward. The ward was acute surgery and Ear nose and throat (ENT). When I arrived at the hospital, I was told to report to the Matron's office in the main foyer. I knocked on the door but there was no answer. I went to the porter's desk and he said she had been called away and left message for me to go straight to the ward. I had no uniform so he showed me where to get one from in the laundry room.

    So, there I was, off the street in a uniform and not challenged at all, no wonder so many bogus doctors get to walk on the wards.

    I worked a full shift without anyone checking my credentials, this time I had them with me but the ward sister said the Matron would check and I had to call back at the office before I went off shift. I enjoyed it on the children's ward, I had not really don't any 'proper 'nursing since I qualified so it felt great.

    So much had changed since I had worked on the ward. The monitoring for a start, when I was asked to attach a Sat's probe post operatively, I had no clue what they meant. When I trained, we assessed the blood oxygen by the colour of a patient's skin, The pallor of the face, and Capillary refill time on the fingers. I didn't trust machines enough to rely on their output only.

It was a nice ward and I loved being back at the hospital again, I felt like a 'proper nurse'. I spent most of my initial bank shifts on there and soon felt like part of the team.

Unlike my training days, everyone addressed each other by their first names, even the name badges had the first name on.

It was almost Christmas and they were having a party for the children with Santa and everything. The ward sister asked me to stay behind to help and also to allow the ward nurses to go home and bring their own children from home. I asked if my children could come too and she said no, because I was just a bank nurse. I was really shocked, and hurt. I felt like an outsider for the first time since returning to the hospital.

Holding back the tears I told her I had to get home for my children so unfortunately, I couldn't stay, she wasn't happy but as she said I was only a bank nurse, why should I care. I avoided that ward after that.

I also worked on the surgical wards, there were two wards adjacent to each other, one was really nice and the other was horrible. The staff were rude and never appreciated anything you did; they gave bank nurses the heavier workload too. Sometimes you only have to spend a short time on a ward to understand why they are short staffed in the first place.

When they called from the bank, I didn't always remember which was which so I made a note in my diary, making sure I didn't work on the nasty one. I guess that is the perks of bank nursing.

The bank got crafty though when I kept declining shifts and booked me for the nice ward, when I got there, I was told it was a mistake and I was wanted on the other ward. I wanted to go home but apparently once you show up you are tied to the shift. I stopped accepting shifts on the surgical ward after that.

I spent almost a year working in Cancer research, I was the lead nurse in Bradford during the clinical trials of Interleukin 3. I was technically employed by Leeds university but paid by the bank. It was just me and a doctor from Leeds , he ran clinics every week in the outpatients department and the patients attended the ward for treatment one day a week.

My role was to monitor baseline observations at each visit and to document any side effects that the patient may have had since the last visit. The patients were also weighed every week using old fashioned manual scales because they were felt to be more accurate. They took some getting used to but I soon became proficient at it. Each patient had their own file and everything was documented in there. My pages were always up to date.

The doctor was supposed to fill in the medical information but he had to be reminded constantly to update things.

There was a set criteria, All the patients were within a certain age group and had a terminal diagnosis , they had to have tried everything and this was a last hope. We had no say in who got the treatment and who didn't

The clinical trials were double blind, the information was sent to the leaders of the programme and the computer decided if they were suitable for the trial, the computer also decided if they got the drug or a placebo. Neither I nor the doctor knew which they got. The medication came in vial A and Vial B

While the drug or placebo was being administered, they had to have constant monitoring and bloods taken every 15 minutes . The doctor put in the cannula and took the bloods, I ran down three flights of stairs with the blood and put it in the spinner in the lab. I ran back upstairs and repeated that every 15 minutes for 2 hours.

The doctor said If I trained to take the bloods it would mean he could get on with the paperwork but I declined, he was so lazy, he wanted me to take the blood from the patient, run down, run back up and repeat as well as doing all the observations. Not a chance !

The patients were really nice, it is surprising that people who don't know if they will live or die make the best of what little time they have left. The ladies were knitting things and selling them to raise funds, the men were always upbeat and it broke my heart every time one of them didn't make it. I would wonder if it was because they got the placebo but I understood the need for it to be a blind trial.

I had to speak to the team every week to give them an update and they were getting annoyed because the doctor wasn't doing his bit. I felt like a nagging wife in the end so when I got pregnant with Nathan I did not go back to that job, I returned to the nursing bank.

I only had the standard 17 weeks off for maternity leave, I returned to work when he was 3 months old. Because I was breast feeding, I could only work short shifts. Being on the bank enabled me to pick and choose.

My favourite ward was the orthopaedic ward, it ticked every box. The staff were nice, I loved orthopaedic nursing and they had six beds dedicated to the children on traction. I learnt a lot about traction care and application of the Thomas splint.

One day I went on shift and there was a woman who lived on my street, she had been hit by a car and had multiple fractures. I knew she had a drug problem and in handover they said she was demanding Morphine and strong pain relief all the time. I didn't know her name before but when I went onto the ward, I recognised her straight away. As soon as she saw me, she was constantly shouting out my name and crying out for drugs, even when I explained I wasn't looking after her she didn't stop. I asked to be moved and was sent to help out down in A and E. I avoided the ward until she had been sent home.

My first time in A and E, I nearly fainted watching a nurse scrub grit out of someone's face. It had been a long time since my short stint during my training. How was I supposed to know she had numbed it first? I made my excuses to go to the toilet and sat with my head between my knees. When I returned, I was so pale she knew what had happened and more or less laughed at me. I spent the remainder of the shift helping out in the minor theatre, snipping stitches and applying dressings, I really enjoyed the shift and it went so fast.

A and E went at a much faster pace than everywhere else and I loved working on adrenaline so after that shift I agreed to do more in the department.

Not long after that the bank decided to allocate set areas to the nurses to give a continuity of care. I had to choose between paediatrics, Orthopaedic and trauma, medical or surgical. I hadn't really worked much on the medical wards so I chose orthopaedics and trauma. The sister on the paediatric ward called me when she heard and was not happy , she said I started on there so should have chosen her ward. I explained I never felt part of the team unlike the other areas so refused to change my mind.

It was in A and E I saw my first cardiac arrest. Apart from the old lady during my training I had never been around with a full-blown crash call. One of the sisters was aware I had never seen this so sat me down on the worktop.

"Don't move, just watch, don't fetch anything and don't leave the room, just watch" she said.

So, I sat on the worktop like a gnome without a fishing rod just watching. I was in Awe, it was like a well-oiled machine, everyone knew their role and just got on with it. No one was panicking and I had never seen anything as organised in my life, I never imagined I would be that efficient. I realised at that moment I needed to stay there.

I still did some shifts on the orthopaedic ward initially but that soon petered out until I was virtually full time in A and E.

My husband worked away a lot so my shifts worked around his schedule well. I stayed home on the days he was away and worked when he was home. Most of the shifts were unsocial too so that helped with the financial side of things.

My mum helped a lot with child care too and when she sold her house, she moved in with us full time.

Chapter 7

"You'll Be Right"

When a part time job became available in A and E, I applied straight away. The role was only a D grade but as my experience was limited, I didn't mind, I saw an opportunity to progress and I loved the work there.

I learnt how to apply back slabs and manipulate simple fractures, reducing dislocations and I even trained to undertake wound suturing, I also attended a 3-day IV skills programme, learning about administering IV drugs, cannulation and phlebotomy, I really felt over time I was progressing and ready to take on a senior role. I applied for an E grade but was refused unless I went full time.

"You are not dedicated to the role if you cannot work full time" I was told

"But I have a young family it is impossible, what about Job sharing? "I suggested

"There is no one suitable to job share at this time so I need someone full time"

I did ask my friend Lorraine who had just converted to Registered nurse to job share with me but she didn't feel ready to take on an E grade so soon. So that was it, I had to accept I was a D grade for a while at least.

I tried not to let it affect me, after all I loved my job.

One of the regular attenders was a cousin of my husband, he was an alcoholic and had a reputation for being aggressive, a lot of the staff were scared of him. The first time I saw him my husband had come to collect me and saw him in the waiting area, he told him to behave and he promised he would, he told him who I was and said if he ever gave me grief, he would come looking for him. He was always really polite to me after that.

He came in one day after having a fit but when he came round, he was refusing to have his cannula removed, he also lit a cigarette and was drinking from a can of Cider. I was asked to try persuade him so I went into the resus room. I took his cigarette off him and run it under the tap, I told him it was dangerous with the oxygen and he seemed to accept that, he still refused to have his cannula out so I took his cider off him off him

" Hey that's mine !"

" Yeah, and the cannula is mine, you give me my cannula and I will give you your cider back"

" Fair swap" he said and sat down and let me take his cannula out.

Working on Triage was the best. It made me laugh when school 'friends 'would come in with their kid's expecting favouritism. Often people who had bullied me or not really what I would call a friend. I would explain how the system worked and priority was given to those who needed the most urgent care and not people who were family and friends.

One woman with 5 kids came regularly and asked every time, I hated her at school so not sure why she would assume she was a friend. She moved to a house near me and when she found out where I lived, she even started bringing her kids to the house for treatment. Often, I would tell her to put a plaster on or go see her G.P. Some people just can't take a hint.

A and E always has , and always will be abused, genuine accidents and emergencies are delayed because of people who feel that A and E is a substitute for their GP. When they would complain that the treatment the GP gave didn't work and that is why they were there I would respond with

" If you bought a loaf at Morrisons, would you return it to Tesco's if it was mouldy ? Seems to me if the treatment the GP offered didn't work you should go tell him, so he doesn't give it to someone else with the same problem." It never worked though they were always happy to sit for 4 hours to be told to go back to their GP.

One of the doctors who did shifts in A and E was a GP, he would always insist on seeing his own patients if they dared to attend with something they shouldn't have. He would especially be mad with them if they tried to say their own doctor was not available. If it was not an emergency, he would tell them to go home and make an appointment to see him in the GP surgery, if it was a GP emergency, he would send them to go call the emergency doctor

" I paid for the service so I know you can use it" He would tell them; he would refuse to treat them in A and E.

On Triage we used the Manchester triage system to assess clinical priority. We had a book that included most scenarios and you just followed the relevant path to its conclusion. There were several flow charts you could use but they all worked out with the same result. For example, if someone came with a broken arm it didn't matter if you used the pain or the limb fracture flow chart the result would be the same.

Priority was given on a need basis. The majority of attenders were in the bottom priority and could wait for up to 4 hours. Obviously, this was determined by how busy the department is at the time. Patients were always advised of the category they are assigned at triage to help reduce the amount of people coming to the desk to complain about the wait.

Level	Status	Colour	Time to assessment
1	Immediate	Red	0 minutes
2	Very urgent	Orange	10 minutes
3	Urgent	Yellow	60 minutes
4	Standard	Green	120 minutes
5	Non-urgent	Blue	240 minutes

One of the biggest problems working in A and E in Bradford was the racism, not from the staff but from the patients, it came from both sides and it was so frustrating.

On one occasion an Asian man came to the desk enquiring about his wife who was in resus, I took him straight through to the relative's room. On return to the desk, I was bombarded with irate patients asking why he went in first as they had been waiting much longer,

"I bet it was because he was black" A local drunk shouted

"No, it is because he needed to go straight through and I am not allowed to tell you why so please sit back down"

The same would happen if someone white went through first, I hated having to justify myself to people who only had tunnel vision.

One busy Saturday afternoon a guy was constantly at the triage desk, he was shouting about the wait and said all the doctors were hiding and having a coffee, he had seen them going in the resus and assumed it was a coffee room. In fact, they were all trying to resuscitate a sick child.

One of my colleagues got sick of his 'heckling' and took him to the resus room, she opened the door to show the carnage inside

"Would you like to ask the parents if the doctors can take a break to see you first?" She asked

He sheepishly sat down.

Two hours later I was in the minor injuries with the doctor seeing walking wounded and this same guy came in with a finger injury he had for three days

"Sorry about the wait" the doctor apologised as he entered

"No worries doctor, I am sure you have been busy" he replied

I wanted to punch him in the face! Sometimes it is hard being professional in nursing.

I left the room and shouted "FUCK THE FUCK OFF!" to no one in particular in the staff room, everyone understood. (The staff room was far away from the department so I wasn't overheard)

Apparently in A and E you never to lend your pen torch to a Genito-urinary doctor, I learnt the hard way ! A doctor came into the stretcher room one day asking for a pen torch and everyone said they didn't have one, I lent him mine puzzled. The other nurses were laughing when they told me he was using it to shine through someone's scrotum, no wonder they all said no. Oh well a couple of Sterets and it was good as new.

I got a stunning pen torch once given to me from a rep, it was premium quality ,with a heavy black metallic casing and had gold trim around it. I never lent this beauty to anyone. It ended it's life in a bucket in the sluice. I had been assisting with a gastric washout for someone who had taken an overdose, as I bent down to pick up the bucket full with a mix of washout solution, alcohol, vindaloo curry and half-digested paracetamol my pen torch fell out of my top pocket right into the middle of it. I didn't bother washing that one I just threw it away.

We were a great team; everyone had the driest sense of humour too. When the phone rang and a gruff voice asked "what colour knickers are you wearing ?" or telling you to "piss off" you knew exactly who it was, obviously someone was bored in the stretcher room today but it made you smile. ha-ha

Everyone coming to A and E first checked in with registration, they would log a basic diagnosis and send the card to the triage desk. We would then call the patients from the waiting area and assess where they needed to go, obviously if someone came in with something more serious you could intercept while the relative checked them in, or we would check them in once they were in a more stable condition if they were alone.

Triage could be fun, I loved people watching, trying to guess what was wrong before the card hit your desk , one guy was brought in by a relative and left at the triage desk, I assume while they parked the car. He was wailing so loud and shouting he had hurt his toe. The registration staff shouted across for one of us to get him and sent the card across with "Toe Injury" as a primary diagnosis, we decided he had stubbed his toe and over reacting, when I went over it seems he had mashed his foot in a lawn mower and his wailing was justified, in fact I would have been screaming not wailing !

A young man came in covered in blood and shouted his friend was outside and been stabbed, he then ran out, tipped his 'friend' on the doorstep and drove off. The man was rushed into resus with serious chest wounds.

I was on my day off when I got the call from the police saying they wanted a statement.

" How tall was he ?"

" I can't remember, sorry"

"What was he wearing ?"

" a t shirt and jeans"

What colour was the t shirt ?"

" It was covered in blood; all I saw was red"

" Was the t shirt light or dark ? "

"I don't know, there was a lot of blood"

" Did it look red like on a light t shirt or dark and not that visible ?"

" I guess the t shirt was white because the blood was very red"

" What colour was his hair ? "

" I have no idea, all I saw was the blood, it happened so fast"

This went on for One and a half hours , I came to the conclusion my people watching skills weren't that good after all. After that I tried to be more observant.

This came in handy with one man, he had been brought to A and E by ambulance with a head injury, the ambulancemen left him at my desk. He was pleasantly drunk and seemed bewildered by what happened, he told me he had been at a friend's house playing cards when all of a sudden, the friend had jumped up calling him a paedo and hit him with a hammer. He seemed ok so I sat him in the waiting area.

A little later a man and a boy came asking for him, I assumed it was his son and grandson because they seemed to be happy to see each other. I didn't hear the conversation but I did notice that they had a good relationship.

After an x ray it was found the man had a fractured skull and they admitted him for observation. At some time later he had signed himself out as he felt he was well enough to go home.

The next day he was found dead, the newspaper had the story on the front page with a picture of him asking for information, apparently, he had a bleed due to the head injury so it was a murder investigation. After contacting the A and E I was advised to contact the police. I told them what the man had told me about his friend hitting him with a hammer and they said the man he was with at the time had come to the A and E and did I see them. This time I was able to give a good description of the people with him and it turned out the man was the one with the hammer and the child was the one he was being accused of being a paedo with. I was confused, they seemed so happy to see each other. At the time I honestly thought it was his son and grandson. Just goes to show everything is not always as it seems.

    One weekend a riot broke out in the waiting area, it was terrifying, I was trapped behind the triage desk with nowhere to get out as chairs, tables and even the computer on the desk went flying. It all started over football in the pub, a punch up had caused some men to attend A and E with minor injuries It ended with more men brandishing machetes and baseball bats coming to A and E. The riot police were called and people made as safe as possible. An announcement was made to say the department was closed and to go home and call their GP if concerned or attend another A and E.

    People were actually coming to the desk asking where they should wait as they needed to see the doctor . The sister told them to go home and sit on their sofa as they wouldn't be seen today. She asked how I was and I was shaking

" I think I need some Valium" I said

"Oh, you'll be right" she told me with a grin, and she was right. A quick cuppa and a cig and I was as good as new.

This was the second time I had seen the riot police, the first time one of my colleagues had been walking past the waiting area and seen a guy with a gun sticking out of his back pocket. She alerted the sister in charge and the police were contacted. They told us not to approach him and get as many people out of the waiting area as possible. Next thing I knew the police had arrived and had him surrounded. They told him to put his hands up while one of the police retrieved the gun. Imagine the nurses embarrassment when it turned out to be a cigarette lighter ! The police were really nice about it and said she did the right thing because it might have been a real gun, but I bet they were pissing themselves laughing going back to the station .

The department was often short staffed and the senior sister would call to ask you to do overtime. It always started with " Hello, how are you today ?" and if you had no plans it finished with emotional black mail to do the shift. At one point I had a list of excuses by the phone so I wouldn't be caught off guard. I am pretty sure I wasn't the only one.

There was a beat policeman at the hospital, he had an office near the main entrance, his presence was always appreciated. He wore a cape and bobby's helmet like someone straight out of *The Bill* When he was around there was rarely any trouble, he was much more respected than the modern security guards.

One day he was brought into A and E as a patient. A Passer-by ran in asking for a wheelchair and help as the policeman had collapsed in his car, the triage nurse just pointed to the wheelchairs, He looked so worried I followed him out. When I got to his car, I knew he wasn't going to make it, I called for a porter to get a trolley. He had had a massive cardiac arrest and didn't make it; it was so sad and I felt angry at the way the nurse on triage had reacted. He was one of our own after all.

Things had kicked off at home and I had lost my child care, mum had been living with us to look after the kids but after an outburst from my husband she had moved out.

I spoke to the sister in A and E with a view to leaving but they agreed to give me set shifts to allow me to make alternative arrangements. It meant working a twilight Friday and late shift Saturday and Sunday. This was when my husband was at home so he could look after them.

I had spent some time working in the burn's clinic every week. The sister in there was really nice, I learnt such a lot about wound care from her. When I had to change my shifts, I went to see her, I told her I wouldn't see her again and gave her a hug. The next day she was brought in DOA. I was so upset, I felt honoured that I had at least said goodbye even though that wasn't what I meant.

At one of the staff meetings someone brought up the fact that some people got set shifts and it wasn't fair on the others, I went to speak to the sister and ask if she meant me. " Hell, no" she said " when you are on holiday, I have to fight to get anyone to do your shifts, and the first one who moans will get them every week until they complain"

I discovered what the 'emergency trolley' was for that I set up every night on the gynae ward. A lady came into A and E and she had a miscarriage, both of the resus rooms were full and she was waiting to see the gynae doctor. The poor lady was on a trolley in the corridor, she was bleeding so much it was running off the side of the trolley, I had never seen anything like it in my life. Her English was very poor and all she kept saying was "my baby", we all felt so bad for her, it is hard enough to lose your baby but to not understand what is going on was harder, she just kept crying and crying" my baby " she was asking for her husband but he did not come with her when she arrived. The registration staff managed to get a telephone number for her husband and I called him, he spoke good English but said he was working and he could not come. He asked about the baby. I told him that unfortunately she had lost the baby and was bleeding quite heavily, I pleaded with him to come.

" No, not that baby, we have a daughter at home"

" Well can you go home and get her ? Is there someone at home with her?"

" No, I told you I am working, can't you go get her ?"

I was shocked and I didn't know what to do, I knew I could not leave a baby alone at home, I called the ambulance service but they had no one available for over an hour so after discussing it with the sister in charge one of my colleagues and I went in her car to retrieve her. The house was only 5 minutes away from the hospital, we both had to go so I could hold her on my knee while my colleague was driving.

When we got to the house the door had been left open, there was no one at home. We walked around the house and found the toddler fast asleep in her cot upstairs, she had an open fire in her room, she was covered in blankets and a cot quilt and she was roasting hot. I shuddered thinking about what could have happened if she had been left much longer. I wrapped her in her baby blanket and we took her back to the A and E department.

We got a message to the ward where mum had been admitted to let her know her daughter was safe. The Matron arranged for the toddler to be admitted to the children's ward overnight as a place of safety. I still could not believe her daddy thought driving a taxi was more important than the health of his wife or safety of his baby.

When I got pregnant the third time I had to finish early on maternity leave because I only got 17 weeks maternity pay and if you were sick any time within the last 11 weeks of pregnancy you had to start you leave then. I was suffering bad migraines in my third trimester and it was impossible for me to continue working.

That meant Tiffany was only 6 weeks old when I returned to work. Once again, I was still breast feeding but my babysitter was training to be a nursery nurse and was happy to look after the children when my husband was at work. I would leave expressed milk and once again worked shorter shifts, I used annual leave to make up the hours, we rarely went anywhere anyway so I had plenty to spare.

The hardest part of going back so early was the let-down reflex, when your baby cries your boobs fill with milk in preparation for a feed, the thing is it doesn't have to be your baby crying to set it off, and in A and E there are quite a lot of crying babies over the course of a shift, I would have to go into the toilets and express the milk to stop it oozing through my uniform . Luckily at that time you could start weaning babies from 6 to 8 weeks so it wasn't long before she wasn't feeding at all during the day, just for comfort at bedtime and I got back to my normal routine.

They built a beautiful Paediatric department , themed around a ship, the triage desk was built like the bough of a ship. The patients started to be divided into adults and children, the cut off age was 16 years, but between 12 and 16 they had a choice of which department they were seen in, some said whichever is fastest which would annoy me but I never gave them an answer to that as A and E was the one department where everything can change in seconds.

If a child looked at their mum for a decision, I would advise them to use the children's department.

I loved working in the children's area, I took charge most shifts too, I asked about a promotion and was told that they would need a paediatric nurse to run the department and I was general trained.

When nurse training started to branch off in the 1990's General nurses would soon be reimagined as adult nurses which I found a great insult. I was no more a dedicated adult nurse than I was a mental health nurse. I trained in all areas and felt I should have the choice of which speciality to take based on experience but unfortunately it was not my decision.

I was told if I wanted to stay working in the paediatric area, I would have to convert to a paediatric nurse otherwise I would be based in the adult A and E.

At my next personal review, I asked if I could undertake the conversion and was told there were no available spaces but I could do the coronary care course if I wanted. I had no interest in coronary care so I was left "to think about it"

I had spent 11 years in A and E and still only a D grade, how do you explain how you were in the same place for all that time and still only on a basic level. I am not sure refusing to work full time was a good excuse

I went into the staff room and I was in tears, One of the Junior sisters came in and asked what was wrong. I told her I was fed up of my future being decided by other people all the time and I had wanted to do my paediatric conversion but was told no.

She told me to contact a lady in the university and told me that she would arrange a pathway for me to enable me to progress. I was so grateful and agreed to call the next day.

I made an appointment with the university lecturer and told them how I felt held back and that pretty soon I would be stuck in the adult department even after virtually running the paeds department for years.

The tutor told me that every year 4 places were allocated on the paediatric conversion course to A and E, two in April and two in September but they never filled them. I was shocked, I had never heard that before. The course was open learning and involved attending college one day a week and organising placements during the course to cover all areas of paediatric care. I would still be based in A and E but they had to give me time off for study and for other placements.

The tutor asked about my training and development and I explained that most of my training had been in -house and that my original training was traditional in a school of nursing. I was advised to undertake the facilitating nursing course (ENB 998. aka mentorship course) to get me used to university level study before the conversion course started. I was told I had a provisional place booked on both courses and all I needed was my manager's signature.

I made an appointment to see the level 3 manager and went armed with the forms. He asked if they knew 'downstairs' that I wanted to do the courses and I said yes, well, they did know, he didn't ask if they agreed so I wasn't lying. I felt bad going behind her back but I felt she was deliberately holding me back because I refused to work full time.

The facilitating nursing course started in 1999 and took me into the millennium. I was still working in the department with one day a month off for the course work.

My regular Friday twilight shift finished at midnight but everyone who worked beyond midnight on the night of the Millennium or on the 1st of January got an extra pay out, so many people had decided to work late, managers especially, whoever heard of a manager hanging around at 2 am on New Year's Eve before ?

The sister changed my shift from four until midnight to five until one am so I wouldn't miss out, she felt there may be issues after midnight so better I stayed behind 'just in case '

There was such a lot of hype on TV and in the papers too and there was fear the A and E computers may go down at midnight and too many people attending due to celebrations etc. but in reality, the scaremongering kept people indoors.

One drunk guy came in with a cut on his hand early in the evening, the department was dead so I took him through to the stretcher area to take a look at his cut while his girlfriend went to register him at the desk. In the stretcher room there was a CCTV screen where you could see the waiting area. One of my colleagues saw the girl going to the desk on the screen.

" My God, look at the state of **that**" she said "she forgot to put her skirt on by the look of it "

I was trying to get her attention as she obviously didn't see me bring the guy through.

"Cough, cough"

"I mean, who wears a skirt that bloody short?" She continued

"Cough,cough"

The guy did not realise, thankfully he was too drunk. I had to go over to her to whisper in her ear "it is *His* girlfriend"

" Oops!" she said laughing as she left the room glancing in his direction just as his girlfriend came staggering in, make up all smeared and dress riding up her backside

I loved the twilight shift; everyone went out looking fab and they would come in pissed later looking wrecked and still think they look as hot as they did when they set out.

At midnight there was only one patient in the department, a 16-year-old who had got drunk and dumped by her friends in the middle of Shipley, she just needed to sleep it off while waiting for her parents to arrive so I got to go home a little earlier.

The department had more managers and senior staff than I had ever seen, and for what ? An extra few quid in their pay packet?

Every member of staff in A and E got a gift for the millennium, unfortunately they had asked one of the secretaries to go get the gifts , something with a message on , a keepsake.

We all thought a pen, scissors, a watch, maybe even a plaque but she bought letter openers ! I don't know many nurses or doctors who have a use for a dedicated letter opener but I kept it anyway.

I completed the Facilitating nursing course ; it was difficult to adjust to university after the spoon-fed method of learning I was used to. There was a lot of research involved and basically quoting everyone else, there was very little room for common sense, everything was evidence based and I now understood why some students seemed more academically focused and many lacked basic nursing skills or common sense.

I started to mentor students in the new year but I was limited to the time I could dedicate to them. I was only part time and also started working on the paediatric conversion course so shared the role with other nurses.

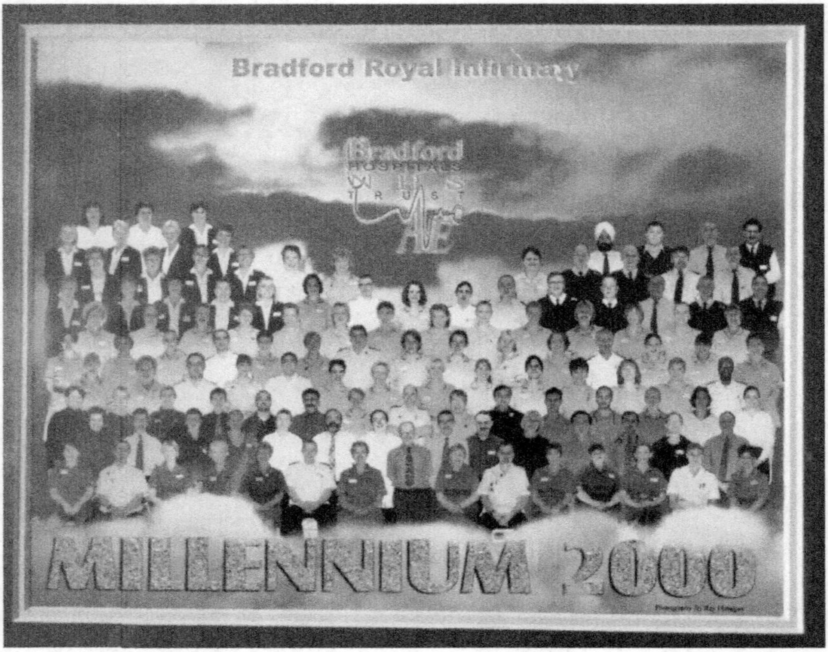
Bradford Royal Infirmary
Bradford
MILLENNIUM 2000

Chapter 8

Paediatric Conversion

The first day in university for the conversion course blew my mind. The course was open learning and I was responsible for arranging my own placements and providing evidence of practice.

There was an accompanying booklet that seemed never ending and each page had questions and things I needed to complete in just 18 months, what the hell ??? There were assessments at the end of each term and competencies that had to be in the form of a 2000-word essay for every placement , as well as areas for the staff to complete as evidence.

I got home and was in tears, I couldn't see how I could possibly complete all this in just 18 months, I didn't even understand half of the jargon in it.

Once I calmed down, I took a closer look, I got myself a sheet of paper and went through the booklet page by page. I wrote down all the questions and competencies I need to complete translating into 'normal' language as I went. When I finished, I realised it only filled one A4 sheet and it looked a lot less daunting, "piece of piss" I thought and felt much better about it all.

I spent the next few days ringing around and arranging placements where necessary. They had to coincide with the theory in that area so I wanted to get in quick so I didn't miss out on a placement. I needn't have worried though because although the course was based in Bradford a lot of the students were from all over the country and there were just me and Bernadette from Bradford.

A and E was easy as we both worked there anyway. The children's wards were spread out a little, some at St Luke's hospital and some at BRI. For every placement I arranged I had to have a police check, it wasn't so bad though as the cost was all part of the course.

I arranged my first placement on the medical ward at St Luke's, the staff were very welcoming and I settled in well. It was only for two weeks but I learnt a lot about different syndromes, enough to know there were way too many to remember and it wasn't for me. It was summertime and we got to take the children outside in the little play area. On a particularly nice day One of the nurses asked her husband to bring in a portable BBQ for when she was on her break. We sat outside on the grass and had burgers for tea.

I was a little sad to leave there and I got a great leaving gift too, headlice ! I became neurotic about them after that, I would scrape my scalp sore every day checking .

My Surgical placement was on the General surgery and orthopaedic ward, I dodged a bullet there as it meant I didn't have to return to the ENT ward and face the sister who was unhappy with me.

The ward had a lovely sunny atmosphere, a nightingale ward with 4 side rooms, the side rooms were used for infectious patients or for those who needed to be reverse barrier nursed, children who had cancer, children with burns and those who had cleft palate surgery. Bradford Royal Infirmary was the main centre for cleft palate surgery so there was a child in there most of the time.

The only issue I had was the placement for PHDU as there wasn't one in Bradford at that time. The competencies meant I had to look after a child that was intubated or sedated. I asked in Uni if I could use my experience in A and E but they said no it had to be specific in PHDU or PICU.

The placements were based on hours not days / weeks so I managed to arrange two full weekends in Leeds, my husband dropped me off on the Saturday morning but I needed to get the train back. I didn't realise how close to the train station the hospital was so I booked a taxi. The taxi went all the way around Leeds to get there and cost a fortune. I could see the hospital buildings from the station and asked why he had taken such a long way around; he explained it was a one-way system. I asked why he didn't tell me it was so close to walk and he just shrugged and said I booked the taxi it was none of his business.

The taxi had taken so long I missed my train, so on the Sunday I asked my husband to pick me up. It was so hard working such long days after only working short shifts for a long time and going home to study and take care of three children was draining. Thank goodness it was only two weekends. It wasn't a very nice place to work either, the staff were very standoffish , the slow pace made it even more tiring. Bernie asked if she could just do the one weekend as she found it hard going and university said that was ok, wish I had thought of that !

Not all the placements were hospital based, I arranged to visit one evening at the local youth centre to do some health promotion. I made a display of road safety posters and leaflets. I think the guy running it must have thought I was some kind of play leader because at one point he gave me a walkie talkie and buggered off upstairs to play football with some of the older kids leaving me in charge downstairs.

I arranged a placement at the local day nursery and while I was there, I did another health promotion session on hand washing with the preschool children. It involved covering their hands with green paint and then perfecting the technique to get it all off, the nursery kept picture diaries for every special activity and I made a book with photos of the children at different stages for the nursery to keep, I also made a copy for my evidence with written permission from the parents.

Getting the formula of the paint right so it washed off instead of permanently staining their hands was the biggest challenge. In the end I mixed the paint with baby shampoo so it washed off easily and no tears if they got it in their eyes (and no angry parents if it went on their clothes)

My daughter was in reception and she told her teacher about the hand washing book, when the teacher saw me, she asked me if I would do the same in their reception classes. I arranged to go for a morning but ended up staying all day as each teacher asked me to do their class too.

4-year-olds are so funny. To make the sessions easier I took 5 children at a time into the cloakroom, On the left was the boys and on the right the girls. Each sink had 5 taps and the teacher said the girls cloakroom was probably the best of the two.

" Miss, Miss, he isn't allowed in here " the girls kept telling me, at every session, the boys would wait and were unsure of what to do. When they dared to venture in the girls were pushing them out again. In the end I took them in groups of just girls or just boys.

I was provided with regular coffees and lunch while I was there and it was great to have an insight in my children's day. The boys often came home with nasty grass stains on their shirts, I found out it was because they raced down the grass hill on their bellies encouraged by the teachers !

The competencies weren't so hard once I got used to it and often, I would write them in advance to make sure they were never late. I would lay in bed at night and think about them so much I often wrote them at 3 or 4 am when there were less distractions. The kids were at school through the day and my husband was at work so I could always catch up on my sleep with an afternoon nap.

I scraped through the written work by the skin of my teeth but Bernie got mad if she didn't get an A in her assignments, I told her at the end of the day a pass is a pass and when she qualifies it won't say "by the way she only got a B+ in one of her assignments" on her name badge.

At the end of the course, we all got a print out of all the names of the people on the course and which hospital they came from in case we wanted to keep in touch, as we only saw each other once a month and for the occasional group work, I never bothered.

After qualifying most of the nurses on the course had been promised an upgrade, not us though, Neither Bernie nor myself were given an upgrade and even though I worked most of my shifts in charge of the children's area they still didn't acknowledge my worth.

The Senior sister had retired and We now had a charge nurse in the department, I had my annual review and told him if I didn't get an E grade after this then I would leave, I could not hold my head up knowing they were keeping me down for so long

" You won't leave" he said laughing " you have been here way too long"

When I left that meeting, I started looking for other positions, an E grade was advertised for the children's department so I applied right away. I was told there and then in my interview that I had got the job, I was even asked what speciality I would like. I asked if I could work on the surgical ward and he said yes, I was told I would need a police check as I was moving areas but that would be up to 6 weeks, I should be able to start on the ward in the new year.

" When do I give my notice ?"

" You don't need to it is a transfer so I will arrange it all don't worry "

It was a shame really, I wanted to put it in the charge nurses' Christmas card.

When he did find out it was only a week before I started on the ward

" When were you going to tell me then ?"

" I did but you didn't believe me, I don't need to give my notice according to the manager as it is a transfer" I didn't feel guilty at all, disappointed but not guilty.

Chapter 9

Moving Up In The World

A and E was in the basement of the hospital, I never really saw anyone in the main hospital unless I did a transfer to the ward and even that was limited contact as you had to get back to the department ASAP, often to return equipment or help the porter with the trolley. We even had our breaks in the staff room as all breaks were paid 'on call'

When I moved up to ward 2 the children's surgical ward, it was so different from the children's ward I had worked on all those years ago in the ENT block, the sister had long since retired and all the surgical specialities had merged. That ward was now paediatric medicine, they had moved across from St Luke's hospital

Although the surgical patients and staff had merged, there was still a faint trace of the two teams. The nurses from the ENT ward wore blue polo shirts and those from the orthopaedic and general surgery wore red. The sister on the ward informed me that they would all be wearing the blue polo shirt eventually so that is what I wore. I preferred the red but I suppose it made sense to integrate the staff better by keeping the same colour for all.

The whole dynamics of nursing had changed, students seemed very laid back and chatty, they were a far cry from the nursing school student nurses and more like the general students sometimes a little too laid back, I overheard one of them call the Charge nurse a 'knob head' one day and I was pretty shocked. I know he could be a bit of a Joker but that was a little too familiar and disrespectful in my opinion. He didn't say anything which was an even bigger shock.

On one of my first shifts, I was allocated 4 children who had been to theatre for their tonsils out, they were all sleeping in the same area so it was easy to move from one to the other to take their observations, initially very frequently but gradually increasing the time in-between. One of the mums had not been for anything to eat so she asked me to sit with her daughter in case she woke up. I sat in the comfy chair next to the bed and watched home and away while she slept. I couldn't believe the change in pace from A and E. The charge nurse from A and E came up to the ward to see me on that same day

" How are you settling in ?"
" Good thanks"

" I was thinking, maybe we were a bit quick to refuse you an E grade and how would you feel if we reconsidered ?"

" How are you planning that ? after all it is a full-time nurse you want"

" We decided to offer you the 24 hours and put the other 16 hours to the bank until you felt able to go full time"

" I have just sat and watched home and away for more money than I got working my arse off and you really think I plan on coming back ? It is too late; I have begged for long enough and now I am happy where I am"

He wasn't happy but, in the end, I agreed to work some bank shifts occasionally to 'keep my hand in' and that seemed to please him.

Inside I was seething, I was happy on here now, but why did they wait for me to leave to offer me the position ?

Each child that was admitted had a relevant care plan relating to their reason for admission, it wasn't very personal and sometimes things could be easily missed. Personal cares weren't included on that and on admission the care plan should be adjusted accordingly, not everyone did that though. A lot of notes just had the standard print out signed at the bottom with nothing added.

In my first week I was looking after an 8-year-old boy with a knee infection. His mum rarely visited and so he relied on nursing staff for all his cares. In the evening I went to get him ready for bed, I took a washbowl and got him some clean pyjamas out, as I looked in his locker for a toothbrush his Auntie came to visit. I asked if he had a toothbrush and he got one out of the drawer, it was brand new in the box. His Auntie told me she bought that when he was admitted 2 weeks ago. He said No one had asked him to clean his teeth for two weeks ! All I could do at that point was apologise and reassure his auntie that I would address it straight away.

As a mum of young boys, I know they only clean their teeth when told to . I was disgusted that not one nurse had asked him. I wrote it in his care plan in capital letters and brought it to the attention of the sister in charge.

One nightshift I was in handover at the start of my shift and a Mum came to the office door, she informed me she was going home but her son needed the toilet. I had been allocated to look after him and it had been handed over, he had his tonsils out that morning. I reassured mum I was out on the ward soon and would make it a priority.

When I went out on the ward, I went to see the boy and tried to get him up to go to the toilet. He said he couldn't get up

" But you had your tonsils out this morning you should be able to get up now"

" No, I have cerebral palsy" he said laughing.

I didn't find it funny at all, I felt so bad for insisting, maybe that was something important they should have handed over but his care plan said he was a tonsillectomy.

After that I made sure I wrote out all my care plans tailored to the child and not just the diagnosis.

Nightshifts on the children's ward could be hectic if the children woke up distressed. On a nightingale ward if one was awake, everyone was awake. The sluice was in the middle of the ward and would bang if anyone let it go or if a window was open. We tied all kinds of things to the handles but found the best thing was an old-fashioned sanitary towel, the ones with loops. One loop on one side of the door and one on the other, there was just enough padding to stop the bang and we could still have it almost closed at night. There were some strange looks on the odd occasion I forgot to take it off in the morning

There were a lot of children admitted with abdominal pain , the Drs would treat this as an appendicitis unless otherwise proven. Bloods were taken on arrival and I was trained to cannulate and take blood when I was in A and E so I could sort this while we waited for the doctor to arrive. Sometimes we even had the results before the doctor got there. If the tests were positive, they were taken to theatre straight away or as soon as a space was available.

Not all Abdominal pain is an emergency, it is often due to poor diet or constipation and teenage girls didn't always cope well with period pains.

Some older children would develop pain on a Monday morning and that could be trebled on exam days. There were children who would be running around happily all day and lay like dying ducks when the doctor or the parents were there.

No parent wants to admit their child is faking or not quite as bad as they say so they all assume it is the appendix, some parents are that adamant the Drs would agree take the child to theatre to take a look, while they were there, they removed the appendix rather than go back in at a later date.

We did get regular attenders and we had to be aware of other concerns that manifest themselves as abdominal pain: Munchausen by proxy, child abuse and simple anxiety.

One girl kept coming to the ward, she had a poor diet and was obese. Her mum was adamant that it was her appendix despite all the tests coming back normal. She said her appendix burst when she was a child and no one believed her because the tests were normal. This girl had every test possible, she even had scans which were conclusive. Her mum always brought her at night screaming in pain, as soon as her mum left the ward she was laughing and joking and slept like a baby. She would tell her mum the staff left her in agony all night despite being observed sleeping by everyone on a nightingale ward.

 On one occasion the girl had the numbing cream applied to her hands for her blood test, mum refused a cannula and insisted the doctor took the blood test, we called the doctor to the ward and it was a new doctor, as she removed the cover on the numbing cream a little splashed up towards the girls face, the mum became hysterical, she rubbed the girls eye repeatedly with a paper towel making it red and started shouting at the doctor, telling her how stupid she was and to get a proper doctor, the doctor went into the treatment room and she was crying. I told the mother she was being ridiculous and the cream at worse would make her daughters skin numb, it didn't go in her eye and the redness was caused by the mother rubbing it. She then started shouting at me and wanted to speak to the person in charge

" I am the person in charge" I told her

" There must be someone more important than you" she screamed in my face.

The mother then walked over to the child's bedside opposite the nurse's desk and was seen to be using the patient telephone, shortly after that the ward phone rang. It was the operator, she told me she had an irate woman on the phone who wanted to speak to the person in charge. I asked her to put me through

" You might want to put down the phone and speak to me in person" I said looking directly at her.

She slammed down the phone. I called the bed manager and asked if she could come and speak to this mother and she said she was really busy and to just fill out an incident report and get the Ward sister to speak to her the next day.

I wrote that many incident reports on that ward someone wrote my name on the front of the incident book ha-ha

After several admissions the doctors decided the only way to stop them coming to the ward was to take out her appendix, she was scheduled for theatre the next day, I have never in my whole career seen a mother and child so happy at the thought of having surgery.

As suspected the appendix was normal. The mother was told the results and advised to see her GP if the pain re occurred. That night I felt sad for the girl as she was in obvious pain for the first time. In the same breath I was relieved she wouldn't be back, or rather her mother wouldn't be.

There was a distinct difference in the way surgical nurses were treat by management compared to those on the medical ward. It didn't matter what level of staff there were if there was a shortfall on the medical ward someone had to go over and help, even leaving their own colleagues struggling.

On one particular shift I was asked to go help on the other ward and I had 5 patients to hand over to my colleagues, this was in addition to their own patients, I left the ward with 2 nurses and 16 children.

It was 1 pm and I had gone straight after my lunchbreak. The medical ward seemed calm when I got there, way calmer than the ward I left. After handover I calculated maybe three patients to each nurse, I was given just 2 patients to look after. One was virtually discharged and waiting to be collected when his mum finished work at 5pm, the other was not on the ward and was returning at 5:30pm for IV antibiotics.

"Is that it ?"

" What do you mean " she said looking genuinely puzzled.

" I have just handed a greater workload over to my colleagues to come here and help, it doesn't seem like you need any help"

" Well, we can soon find you something to do, maybe do some cleaning or something while you wait?"

As she said that the sister from the surgical ward appeared, she had been in the pre op clinic and heard what had been said, she asked me to accompany her into the pre op office.

" Just wait it out" she said " I know it is frustrating but it is out of our hands"

I was furious, I just moped around all afternoon doing nothing until the child came back for his IV's. I then asked if I could go back to cover the girls for break and was told no, I would have to stay for the shift.

At 6 pm I was sent for break " Don't rush back, you could probably take an hour if you want " she said

WTF ? I went over to my own ward for my break and let the other girls have a break, they were so busy I felt guilty, even though it wasn't my fault.

This was not an isolated incident either, it happened so often people were dreading getting moved. Each time I was on shift I filled an incident report in but I never got feedback and no one ever did anything about it.

We used to do all our mandatory training days in B block at St Luke's Hospital, it brought back lots of happy memories. The ward layout on the training floor was just like C3 that I had worked on when I was volunteering . The block was not in use as a ward anymore and the ground floor windows were blacked out. They used to film *The Royal* in there and often on a study day you got to see the film crew outside, I even saw Wendy Craig one day, it was surreal seeing her there in the 'old school' uniform, complete with cape. They didn't do any of the outside filming there so they were just hanging around between sets, I guess. I loved that programme!

In 2004 the agenda for change came in, it meant for annual leave and sickness we would get paid the same unsocial pay we would have got if we had been working. Everyone was looking forward to the backpay for the unsocial hours and sickness pay, there was talk it could amount to thousands for some people. I was never off sick so I got less than £200, I was not amused because so many who had been off sick all the time got a right tidy sum, the ward manager included !

The ward was almost always short staffed, the evenings and nights were the worst, when there was no management around to intervene. Nobody wanted to work overtime because they never knew if they would get moved so it was hard to cover the shift if anyone was off sick.

I was on a late shift and the ward was almost full, there was myself and two other nurses on the ward. One of the nurses had escorted a patient to theatre, one was in a side room cleaning up a child who vomited and I was in the main ward feeding a baby.

The anaesthetist came to see a child he was taking to theatre, He asked me to escort him but I said I couldn't as I was busy and there was no one else on the ward. He was not impressed; he said the ward was unsafe and he didn't even feel happy taking another child to theatre

"What if a child goes 'off' while there is only you here?" He asked

" Well, I put the baby back to bed to cry for food and deal with the emergency" I told him " This is getting the norm to be honest and as soon as I get chance, I will fill in another incident report"

" Where is the book ?" he asked " I will fill one in for you !"

The next morning, I was called to the office to be told the anaesthetist consultant had filled in an incident report about the ward, I felt like I was being told off for the state of the ward! I was quick to stick up for myself

"I know he did, he borrowed my pen. It wasn't about us it was on my behalf because I didn't have time" But still nothing changed.

That didn't stop my enjoyment on the ward, working with a good team makes all the difference, sometimes when you are really busy it brings the staff closer together.

Things did not end well in my marriage and I had to flee my home to move into a women's refuge in Halifax. I was unable to work for a while and the sister was so supportive. After 6 weeks I returned to the ward and commuted from Halifax every day. It wasn't too bad; the bus was at the end of my street and I could catch the train to speed up my journey. It was harder when the weather was bad.

In the refuge we weren't allowed to leave the children at any time, at first one of the other ladies offered to look after Nathan and Tiffany until it was time for school but the staff got wind and said I shouldn't have asked her because everyone there has their own problems, but I wasn't allowed anyone in for child care either !

In the end I got a child minder, she lived a 30-minute walk away, it was winter and I had to take Tiffany there for 7 am so I could get to work on time. Nathan said he would leave the refuge when we did but did not want to go to a childminder so he would just hang around until school opened, in the end the refuge staff agreed to let him wait in our room for an hour before school on his own, to be fair they wouldn't have known anyway because they didn't start until 9 am.

Tiffany's school was virtually across the road from the refuge so the poor kid had to walk all the way back when it was time for school too.

One day the snow was really heavy but the buses and trains were still running, I got to work a little late and everyone was shocked to see me.

Some of the staff between Halifax and Bradford had called in saying they couldn't get there due to the weather, cars stuck in drive, roads closed etc. Yet I got there on public transport. The manager was not happy and contacted them saying if I could get there so could they. When they arrived on shift, they were not happy with me but I was soon forgiven….I think.

I found out that the school had closed for the day too but the childminder had just kept Tiffany at her house, she didn't bother contacting me because was happy to keep her there to keep her daughter company, she did not charge me for the extra time either.

Nathan sustained a head injury at school one day and I was on my way home when I got the call. I called the childminder to tell her and she said she would meet me from the train and take me to the hospital. She even lent me taxi fare to get back home and kept Tiffany overnight. My life was definitely made easier with the great support I was given.

When I moved out of the refuge after a few months we rented a house in Halifax , Nathan was happy to look after Tiffany for the 3 days a week I was working so I could get back into my usual shifts, I only worked short days so it was only a matter of before school or for a few hours in the evening. When I worked nights, I made sure it was at the weekend and took them to stay at mum's.

I had a good social life on the ward, I got on with virtually everyone and we often had days out and trips away. One of my closest friends was Lisa, we often went to Chiquito's to eye up the sexy waiters, Lisa ordered a pancake dessert once and they brought it looking like a penis with squirty cream coming out of one the end, it looked nothing like the one on the menu and I am sure they did it on purpose, Lisa's face was a picture when she saw him bringing it to the table and we couldn't stop laughing.

Lisa lived in Halifax so she often gave me a lift home too which made things so much easier, she made me laugh though because she always kept her car door locked on my street like I was in some kind of shanty town.

I can't say it was an easy time, the lack of supervision caused Nathan to go off the rails, he got mixed up with a local boy and was rarely attending school. I knew it could not be a permanent solution but at that time it was all I had.

A year after I had left my husband, we had sold the family home. I had been to the nursing congress in Huddersfield, granted I only went for the free pens and free food but there were a lot of Job opportunities there too, they all meant relocating. The one that appealed to me the most was paediatric nursing in Canada. They offered me a nice package for relocation, including free accommodation and free child care for the first 6 months. I brought home a DVD and the kids were buzzing .I spoke to mum about it but she wasn't so happy, she became very upset and said she felt she would never see me or the kids again, Mum had decided a long time ago not to travel abroad as she was afraid of becoming ill away from home. She reminded me I had a new granddaughter too and it would isolate me even more to be in another country. I gave it a lot of thought and she was right I suppose, so I decided against it after all.

  I even looked at houses in the Lake district near my friend Jane but the housing market was not great and those in her village would mean a lengthy journey to get to work, as a non-driver it wasn't viable really and pretty much the same as what I had been doing, commuting on public transport.

  I moved to Hull to be nearer my eldest son Daniel and his family. Initially I thought it would be a good idea to commute but it was harder than I thought.

  Daniel and his wife Vikki stayed at my house bringing my granddaughter with them for 2 nights a week to look after the other two and I stayed at mums in Bradford doing a three shift straight every week I went home on the train after my last shift.

  Nathan was becoming out of control and they had a lot of trouble with the local kids too, one boy even poured petrol in my letterbox threatening to set fire to it. The police were aware of the group , they wore their ASBO's with pride, but there wasn't much they could do without a 24-hour surveillance, there was too much going on after the police went home at night and it was not safe for them to be there, even more so with my granddaughter.

Chapter 10

New Start

Commuting became too hard too but I was applying for jobs everywhere and in every speciality. I applied for a job in A and E in Hull. On the day of my interview, I was ten minutes early, I had been in, had my interview, and back out before my interview time had even arrived, I was shell shocked. The interview did not go well at all. I was asked questions but not given time to answer effectively, every answer was cut short. I am aware of the point system they use for interviews and I am pretty sure the job had already been allocated by the way they did not allow me to tick any boxes. A lot of the interview was based around local policies too so it was impossible for me to know without inside information. I was asked if I wanted feedback and I declined, I was too angry at the time. I didn't get anything wrong in my opinion; I was prevented from getting anything right !

In the end I applied to an agency. I was asked to go for an interview but when I got there it was actually a study day that had been organised. I sat through the day with a really annoying woman next to me, she seemed thick, even the simple computer tasks confused her but hey I helped her out as best I could. When we went for lunch, she introduced herself, she said she was the one interviewing me that day but wanted to kill two birds with one stone so to speak. How unprofessional ! At first, I thought maybe she was acting dumb to see my reaction but no she was just as dumb in the afternoon ha-ha

At the end of the day, she asked me to follow her to the office. It was in the centre of town and quite a trek but I wanted a job so didn't complain. When we got there, she photocopied all my documents , including the mandatory training certificate I had just attained and gave me a run down on the agency. I was given 5 uniforms which I was informed would be taken from my first wage, a further £65 would be taken for the police check that they needed to complete before I would get any shifts.

The pay for the agency staff was from £11 to £32 depending on the level of qualification and the work undertaken. I reckoned as a registered nurse I would be at least somewhere in the middle, maybe £24 an hour

It took another 6 weeks for the police check to come through and then I started to get calls asking me to work in various wards and departments over Hull.

The agency called at the beginning of the week with the shifts available, some woman who barely spoke English and I struggled to understand her most of the time.

My first shift was on a male medical ward. The ward had a variety of rooms and a balcony with beds on. I was allocated the second half of the balcony. There were 5 patients and one empty bed. I was given a brief handover and left to my own devices. I asked another bank nurse what the routine was as it was such a long time since I had worked on an adult ward.

My first job on there turned out to be following a confused man to the toilet picking up turds as they fell out of his trouser leg, such fun !

At 12:00 I was asked if I had given my lady her insulin before lunch

"Lady ? I haven't got a Lady, I thought it was a male ward ?"

"Yes, you got an admission this morning, she is in the day room as we can't put her on the balcony with the men"

WTF ????

" No one told me I had an admission; I don't know anything about her"

" So, who did you think was gonna take her, you only have 5 patients, if it had been a man he would be in your empty bed, don't you check the board ?"

" What board ? don't you people communicate ? I finish at 1 anyway so what is the point of me taking her ?"

I couldn't wait to get off that ward, I wrote a note in my diary never to go back !

My next shift was at Castle Hill hospital, it was a ball ache and two bus rides to get to but apparently the bus to the hospital was free with a name badge.

Castle Hill is like a Maze ; I was to help in the pain clinic there. It took me ages to find the place, in the end a porter took me to the unit. All I had to do was get people onto the bed and check observations, the paperwork was very basic as it was more like an outpatient appointment. The doctors came and cannulated the patients and administered the medication , then they went home. they didn't even have a proper bed ; they were on a wheeled trolley with a basic sheet and blanket. The sister in charge had a specialist role, I was gobsmacked as the care was pretty basic from a nurses perspective!

For one of the bank shifts I was asked to report to the porters desk at Hull Royal for allocation, it was just before Christmas and I had no idea which ward I was on. When I got there, he laughed and said I was about to play a game of Russian roulette as he called the site matron.

The matron came down to the porters desk to meet me and I was taken to a ward in the tower block and just left there, the nurse in charge looked surprised and said they didn't need anyone, she called the matron to ask what I should do and I was sent to another ward and they didn't know why I was there either , after 4 wards and several phone calls the matron sent me to a care of the elderly ward at the back of the hospital.

The building was just like the old ones at St Luke's in Bradford, with the green ornate tiles and high ceilings. The Nurse in charge greeted me with a big hug, "Thank God you are here" she said.

I was sent for a drink and a mince pie before I started as she said she didn't know when I would get another break. The shift basically consisted of turning patients, changing beds and repeat. The staff were so grateful when I finished, they gave me a box of chocolates. I never went there again but I would have been happy to as they were so nice.

At the end of my first month, I had worked around 100 hours but my pay was less than £350.

I called the agency and asked why it was so low and I was told I was on the £11 an hour.

" But surely that is for a care assistant not a staff nurse ? I expected a lot more"

"No, you cannot take charge on the agency so you only get the bottom pay bracket"

What a con !

I was told the uniforms were £50 each, the study day was £150 (that I didn't even book I was just conned into it) I was emergency taxed and the police check was taken off too. Oh, and to add insult to injury they took holiday pay too !

I told her to take me off the books, I was financially better off on the dole.

They kept calling for a while but eventually they took the hint. I never did get my holiday pay back or the so-called emergency tax.

I applied for a job on the children's surgical ward, the same day as my interview I got a call offering me the job, but on the medical ward because they felt my additional skills would be more beneficial there. I was a little disappointed but glad to be back on the children's ward and in a stable position.

Another day another police check, I am surprised it doesn't set sirens off when they type in the query.

Chapter 11

The Dark Side

The wait for the lift was longer than anticipated but as someone who is always early that wasn't a problem, The ward was on the 13th floor so there was no way I was going to walk up the stairs

Walking onto the ward I was feeling so optimistic, I missed being part of a team and I knew that now I could start putting my life back together, the children were now older and it felt ok leaving them alone occasionally for the short time in the evenings. I was only doing short shifts for three days a week.

My first two weeks I was told to wear my own clothes and most of the induction period was spent completing paperwork and in house mandatory training. I was supposed to have a preceptor for this period but the ward manager was off sick and no one else took on that role, by the second week I had completed as much as I could under the circumstances and felt I would be more use in uniform so I asked the person in charge and they agreed for me to start on the ward.

I realised in just a short time that I wasn't welcome. The staff were so tight knit and didn't encourage outsiders at all. It was every man for himself and although each thought the other was so good, behind their backs they were carrying knives.

There was a total lack of respect for senior staff too, Handover was given in the small staff room, there was limited seats and some were sat on the desk or leaning against the windowsill, there were 3 students sat down one morning while the nurse in charge was stood up ! The night nurse came in to handover, a senior staff nurse who had just completed a 12-hour night shift, she looked exhausted and no one let her sit down. In the end I stood up and offered my seat. I cannot imagine as a student even considering taking a seat from a senior nurse.

I was often allocated the hardest patients and my first shift I was given a newly diagnosed diabetic. I asked if there was a protocol as I wasn't sure of the routine.

" Have you never looked after a diabetic before?" I was asked in a sarcastic tone.

" Yes, in A and E and for surgery but never looked after one that needs teaching or stabilising" I replied trying to stay upbeat

"The policies are in the folder above the desk" she said nodded her head in the direction of two large shelves overloaded with files.

Marion, the ward house keeper came to my assistance, she showed me which folder I needed and even pulled out the protocol for me, she gave me a knowing look and smiled. So, it seems they did have one and that is all I had asked for, you would think I was asking for the world. The other staff had gone about their business.

When I went to introduce myself, the child was having breakfast. The dietician had come to visit her and went mad with me because she was eating rice crispies, I didn't give her them and I wasn't aware of what she could and couldn't have at that point but I decided not to rock the boat and just apologised.

A clinical support worker then came to me holding a drug card, she held out her hand to show me two tablets

" Your boy is in pain, I got him some paracetamol , can you just sign for them please?"

" Err no, I don't know what they are, I cannot sign for drugs, are you even allowed in the drug cupboard ?"

" You can see they are paracetamol; can't you just sign ?"

" Sorry no, throw those away , they have been in your hand and I have no clue what they are, I will get some out now, thanks anyway"

BIG mistake, it seems I had upset the whole ward for refusing and they made it as awkward as possible after that day or that is how it felt to me.

On the bus going home I cried, I really thought things were getting better but in fact things were as bad as ever, I needed the job , I needed the money so I knew I had to go back.

I Kept my head down and just got on with things, some days were worse than others but on the whole, I was not happy. Every day I cried going to work and cried going home.

I noticed I was getting a lot of night shifts and it was difficult, , Nathan was OK at home on his own but under 16 so not old enough to be left with Tiff overnight, so I had to send her to Daniel's to be looked after. This was ok on a weekend but not on schooldays.

I asked the nurse doing the off duty if I could work less nights and explained the situation "You knew you had to do nights when you started , it isn't my problem, everyone has to do their share "

I knew I was working more nights than anyone else, most of the time I was in charge with only junior nurses on shift.

On one of these night shifts I had a very sick baby, I spent most of my night stabilising him and asked the other girls to keep an eye on my other patients. They said they would and I had no reason to check up on them. I called the doctor several times to try get the child transferred but they said he was fine on there; they didn't even bother to review him.

      The following morning after handing over to the day team I was called to the office by the acting charge nurse, he told me the girls had been to see him and said they felt unsupported and left alone most of the night. I explained about the sick child and was told I should have delegated ,He said I was responsible for the ward and not just one child. I told him I tried to get the child into PHDU but the doctors refused and the nurses were too junior to take on such a sick baby. When I came on the next night, I was told the baby was transferred to PHDU ten minutes after I left the ward that morning.

      Once again, I was called into the office in the morning. The acting charge nurse said my documentation was not good enough, he told me I had left two children with no observations all night .

      I told him the other nurses had agreed to look after them while I was busy with the baby and I didn't think I needed to check. Apparently, I should have checked; easy said with hindsight but I came from a ward where everyone was professional, supported each other and if someone said they would do something you never had to check up on them.

The charge nurse told me to write more in the notes in future and he would 'touch base' again in a few weeks to see how I was getting on. I told him it was hard to know the right thing to do as I had no support when I started and he allocated one of the senior staff nurses to be my preceptor

A few weeks later I found myself on nights again. I was working with one of the junior nurses and a clinical support worker , everything seemed to be going well until about 2 am and she asked me to give her an update of the patients so she could hand over in the morning, I told her I was handing over and she said she had been contacted prior to her shift and told I was not allowed to take charge. This was complete news to me but to be honest I had got used to the weird ways by now so didn't argue.

When she went for her break a staff nurse, Liz came down from PHDU to cover, I was confused why she was asked to come as the ward wasn't that busy and I did have a clinical support worker. The nurse was just as confused as me, she was under the impression it was a junior nurse she was covering. I told her we were fine if she wanted to go back but she said she has been told that I was under clinical supervision and could not be left alone.

"What ? since when ?" I had not been told anything about this. When she told me that it was two of the day staff that told her , I was shocked, no, devastated. Liz was equally as shocked that I knew nothing about it. She was really nice and said I should Talk to the charge nurse and if I didn't, she would ! I had a feeling I knew her from somewhere but I didn't know where.

I went for my break in a side room and just sat there staring in space, my head was spinning and I just burst into tears, If the window had been open, I would have jumped, I had never felt so low in my life.

The next morning, I stayed behind, I told my preceptor what had happened and she did not know anything about it so suggested we speak to the charge nurse. I was tired but way too angry to go home and go to sleep so decided to speak to him there and then, it was my last night of the week anyway.

I really let rip , I asked why I was on clinical supervision without knowing and he said I wasn't, he had written it as a query before the meeting last week but after talking to me he decided to sit it out

" So, who decided that I wasn't to be left alone ? who did you discuss it with?" I asked

He said he had not spoken to anyone and did not have an answer, the only thing he could think is when accessing the computer to do the off duty the two nurses had accessed my record and took it upon themselves to put things in motion.

" So, what about data protection ? can anyone access my personal records ?"

I told him how nasty the staff had been towards me since I started on there, how I had been a victim of bullying and I cried every day going to work, I told him he was useless and his staff were not a team they were a liability. I asked to be moved to the Surgical ward but he refused and said there was no opening at this time and also my cannulation and blood taking skills were more benefit on the medical ward. That was another thing, I was fully qualified with an NMC certificate in IV skills yet they insisted I did the training for the Hull trust which was basically go through a workbook and have someone witness me do the procedures before signing me off. The nurse who had signed me off wasn't even qualified in IV skills so it had been void and I had to get a nurse specialist to do it. At the time I thought it was funny but with hindsight it was not funny at all that they allowed someone unqualified to do the procedure but tell me I had to retrain.

I knew for a fact there was a nurse on the surgical ward who wanted to be on there and asked if we could swap, he told me they were aware of that but did not want her on their ward, apparently, she was known to them but he didn't go into details just that it was still not possible.

When I had finished my rant, I still didn't have any answers but I told him if he didn't do something About it, I would take it further myself, he assured me he would ensure the staff knew it was a mistake and discipline the nurses responsible.

To be honest I am surprised he didn't fire me but I was angry and tired and I had hit rock bottom.

The next shift one of the two nurses asked to speak to me , she said she was sorry if I felt bullied and she really didn't mean to be like that and I accepted her apology. After that she was a lot nicer towards me. She even offered to look after my dog when I was going on holiday. Things did seem settled for a while but I was never happy on there.

I made a couple of friends and there were some nice people on there, it was just the minority who made it an unpleasant working environment. going on shift was like Russian roulette. It wasn't just me either at the time I started a male staff nurse started too, he was really nice but since qualifying had taken a break so he was quite anxious starting nursing again.

    I walked into the locker room one day and he was there crying and shaking, he said he couldn't face the shift, He had a diary and put different colours in there so he knew what the shift was like, he said it helped him prepare for the bad shifts, on this day he said it was particularly bad with those on shift. Even though I hated it there I tried to keep upbeat and told him I was there if he needed me. The shift wasn't too bad but, in the end, he decided to quit his job rather than suffer the bullying. I wish I could have done the same but in a strange town with no way of supporting myself I had no choice but to stick it out. I have never been so Jealous of anyone in my life .

    A couple of months before Christmas the Charge nurse put up a list of duties that needed covering, everyone had to work part of Christmas or new year so this was seen as the fairest way to do it, on a first come first serve basis. I didn't really have a preference so I put down the shifts I was available, I left Christmas eve blank because we always had a party at Mums on Christmas eve and I didn't want to miss it.

    When the off duty came out, I had been put down for late Christmas eve, early Christmas day, early boxing day, night New Year's Eve and night New Year's Day ! That didn't seem right, everyone commented on how unfair it was. When I approached the charge nurse to query it, he said "Well, someone has to do it and you put your name down "

I explained they were the shifts I was available I didn't expect to get all of them !

He told me it was too late now as everyone had their shifts and it was unlikely, I could swap with anyone, when I got upset, he accused me of being aggressive and asked me to leave.

A few days later he came back to me and said a lot of people had told him it was unfair so as a good will gesture he offered to do my Christmas eve. I still couldn't go to Mum's party as I had to be back for the early Christmas day. Mum was devastated and offered to ring him on my behalf, I knew it was pointless so told her not to bother and I would make sure I was off the following year .

Nathan went across to stay at mum's for Christmas but Tiffany stayed home with me, the other staff said I could take her in for the morning but she wanted to go back to bed when I went to work. I felt awful leaving her , Christmas dinner that year was Southern fried chicken from the freezer.

The ward had a lot of regular attenders and some of the staff did favour them, they hated it when someone new looked after their child or didn't give in to their every whim. One of the parents complained to the nurse in charge and asked for a different nurse, she said I had refused pain relief for her child but at the time it was not due, I had told her I would take it when it was due. She said I gave him tablets and when she asked for medicine, I told her " I haven't got any medicine so tough ! "

This was a downright lie but the nurse took her word over mine. To be perfectly honest I was glad I didn't have to look after him, it wasn't the child, he was sweet, it was the horrible mother .

I met miss B while I was on there too. A child had been transferred from PHDU following an appendicectomy the previous week, the surgical ward had no cubicles and I was told he had been quite sick but ready to be transferred to the ward. The nurse said he could eat and drink and his mum was currently getting him some food from the lunch trolley.

Before the child's mum came back Miss B came to see him, his mum walked in with a Jacket potato and beans. Miss B went mad and started shouting at me

"This is a sick boy, he has just left PHDU why are you allowing him to eat so much? He is a surgical patient not a medical patient !"

" Really ? I didn't get the food, mum just arrived with it, oh and incidentally I am a surgical nurse not a medical nurse but I only know as much as I was told at handover"

" My patients don't have beans, make sure everyone knows in future!" she said as she left the ward

I had to laugh to myself, I liked her, I don't know what it was, maybe like me she doesn't take bullshit and that appealed to my sense of humour.

The other staff seemed scared of her but I wasn't, I would like to think she respected me for that.

The new doctors always amused me, they followed her around like a lost puppy looking terrified and when she wasn't there, they tried to act like they had some kind of authority and we all know the nurses call the shots half the time.

The next time I saw Miss B I was on a night shift, one of the children I was caring for had a very distended abdomen so I called her to assess him. When she came to the ward, I was eating my 'tea', a curry I brought from home. She asked for someone to accompany to her and as per the way staff were on there, they told her I was his nurse and went back to reading their magazines.

I went to see the child with her and when I returned to the desk, she thanked me for my help, she apologised saying it would have been nice if one of the others had got up so I could have my food while it was hot. I think it went straight over their heads because they didn't say anything.

I guess that is because it was a case of 'it is your patient 'all the time, if a child had an infusion and it alarmed, they would rather come and find you rather than attend to it.

I never felt they trusted my judgement either, one day they got a diabetic who needed to go on a sliding scale, at last it was something I could do with my eyes shut so I offered to help. The nurse declined and said she had called someone from PHDU to work it out.

I watched them struggle with something that I found really simple but I didn't care anymore, I was done trying to fit in , I even considered quitting nursing altogether.

Even one of the play specialist had a go at me because I had gone to help a doctor with a cannula and didn't ask for her help, she reported me to the ward manager, after that I asked her every single time, most of the time she refused with some feeble excuse but at least she couldn't go telling tales again. Each time she refused I documented it in the child's notes just in case she felt like lying about it.

I stuck it out for almost three years and the management decided to have a shake up within the paediatric department. Everyone was given a chance to choose the department they wanted but inevitably the management would decide in the end

The form had the three choices like the one you fill in when choosing a school, you had to give a reason for each one to strengthen your case. My response :

1. Surgical ward, most of my experience is in paediatric surgery, I have special skills in orthopaedic care and feel they are wasted on my current ward.
2. Surgical ward, I hate Medicine
3. Surgical ward, I have no experience with babies or neonates.

That'll do !
Thankfully when the decision was made, I had got my first choice

Chapter 12

Coming Out Of The Dark

My first shift on the surgical ward I felt like I had gone home, it was a total contrast to the medical ward. The staff all helped out each other and for the first time in 3 years someone came up to me to ask if I needed any help with anything, I could have cried.

The staff were telling me they were dreading me going on there because of rumours they had heard but apparently, as Hannah put it " I am better for knowing" I am not sure if that was a compliment to be honest ha-ha

There were quite a few 'old school' nurses on there too so they were experienced enough not to have anything to prove.

In my experience children on surgical wards are always happier than those on the medical ward. I suppose it is because most of the time they come in sick and go home well, whereas a lot of children with medical problems come and just get a diagnosis, often with long term implications.

I did struggle with the poor sense of humour in the children though. A 10-year-old child asked how we got the tonsils out,

"Well," I said with a smile "we pull off your head and take them out , then put your head back on" I thought I was being funny but he started screaming he didn't want his head pulling off, his mum was not impressed, oops ! I thought by that age he would get the joke.

There was a 5-year-old that really made me laugh though. He had a circumcision and his mum came to ask for pain relief for him. It was customary to monitor the pain score so we could decide the best pain relief to give. We had a few different pain tools we could choose depending on the child's age and development. I learnt the importance of using the right chart that day. Mum felt he would understand the 0-10 scale.

I showed the little boy the chart and asked him "If 0 was no pain and 10 was really bad pain where is your pain?"

" In My Willy" he said , I think maybe we used the wrong chart even though it did make us all laugh.

It wasn't long before I was making friends and I found it easy falling into my role. Unlike the ward in Bradford the children were collected to go to theatre and brought back to the ward, the difference that meant to time management was incredible.

There were two male nurses on there , both nearing retirement and with a real dry sense of humour; I remember when they changed all the paperwork for no apparent reason and Richard said it was because the new Matron wanted to make a point of doing something to justify her role.

"Deckchairs on the titanic" he said. And I laughed because he was right. I was sad when Richard left, he was always fun to work with.

He had a leaving party when I was off with hip and knee problems prior to my hip replacement surgery, I was dancing and having a great time. Someone had said half joking there didn't seem to be much wrong with my hips or knees. I told her if I could have paracetamol, tramadol and 6 Bacardi's before work I would probably manage through the shift.

John was like the ward patriarch and when he left to retire things were never the same. I loved his dry sense of humour but not so keen on his habit of farting and disappearing before you got hit with the smell. He never denied it when caught out though.

I found I was getting more friends and felt so much happier all round, I would meet people out of work which had been unheard of from the other ward.

One of my best friends was Kerry, she was such a fun person to be around, with her warped sense of humour we were well matched. She would come around to my house often and we would put the world to rights. Kerry had gastric surgery, the same surgery my husband had and her visits soon turned into them two comparing notes and her bringing me her fat clothes as she lost weight!

We often went out for lunch, to the garden centre for a wander or to the cinema. Kerry was a fantastic nurse but her confidence was shot after she made a drug error, it had been under investigation and the management and union were not very supportive. Kerry even asked to be moved out of the clinical area but they refused saying there was no other area available. When Kerry was on shift, she always offered me a lift home.

The last time we worked together it was a late shift, she hadn't taken her car and offered me a Croggy home on her bike instead, I declined. The next day I was given the news that Kerry had had a heart attack and was in Intensive care.

The team were told her family had specifically asked that no one from work visited, I know that her mum blamed the department for the stress she suffered but I was her friend, I was devastated. When the Matron came to give us an update, I was furious when she said she had been to visit. I told her it was unfair I couldn't go yet she could go and I knew for a fact Kerry disliked her.

One of the doctors suggested I get out of uniform and visit anyway but I really wasn't in the frame of mind anyway that day.

The next day Kerry died; I was heartbroken but also angry that I never got to say goodbye.

I wrote to Kerry's mum and asked if I could go to the funeral and she said of course I could. It turned out that what she had said was she did not want any of the management going to visit and that of course she knew she had friends that would want to go to the funeral. Kerry had only just celebrated her 40th birthday so the whole ward was in shock.

After we lost Kerry weird things happened on the ward and I would blame her: things would go missing and reappear 5 minutes later, on one night shift a chair came out of nowhere into the middle of the corridor, there was no one around

"Pack it in Kerry, you are not funny" I would say laughing.

We lost another nurse that year too , I wasn't that close to Heidi but she was a lovely person and I enjoyed her company on many a night shift.

Hannah and Chris were best friends and I found I had so much in common with them.

I invited them round to my house for Hannah's birthday and we had egg and chips, before long I had a reputation for the best egg and chips and everyone wanted them when they came. I wouldn't care I can cook other things too.

A lot of the nurses would bring baking from home or packets of biscuits to share at coffee time. I would often bake for the ward too; I enjoy baking and would take in cakes and buns for the staff. Jackie the ward clerk was a fan of my jam and coconut topped cake or buns and would request them if she knew I was baking at all.

After I took cake on a night shift John came in the next night with brownies he bought from the supermarket,

" Here I made you a cake " he said laughing.

I started to have problems with my knees and hips and had some time off sick, almost a year in fact having knee washouts and two hip replacements. (One a revision of my first hip replacement)

Around 5 months after my last hip replacement /The manager at the time called me at home to ask when I was coming back, yes not to ask how I was, just when was I returning. I explained I would return when the physio was happy with my progress and at that time I was still walking with a stick. She advised me I would soon be on half pay as if that would motivate me to walk better. She then said for me to not rush back as the staff would not be able to 'carry me' and once back on the ward I would be expected to fulfil my role.

I had to have an appointment with occupational health before returning to the ward, the doctor insisted I took a slow return and minimise the walking , so no transfers.

When I did return to the ward they had moved over to a different unit. I was on phased return initially and used that time to get up to date on my mandatory training.

The new ward was really nice, a little confusing at first but once I got the map in my head, I was fine. The dynamics on the ward had changed as some of the older nurses had left and new nurses started, they all seemed nice and fit well into the team. There were a couple who weren't team players but they soon left to work elsewhere.

A lot of the nurses were asking about learning to do cannulas and bloods but were sent to Paediatric outpatients for it. The fact I was fully trained, and had done an annual update as a facilitator went right over management heads. For some reason they still had it stuck that I had trained somewhere else, I kept a folder for the IV updates and all my documentation was kept in there. During the move the folder had gone missing and the new sister did not believe I had completed the necessary training. The funniest part of it was she was the one who signed it !

I even searched the loft to see if maybe I had put it with my paperwork, I didn't find it but I did find the list from the conversion course and saw Liz the PHDU nurses name on there, so that is where I knew her from . I told her the next time we worked together and she said she thought she knew me from somewhere too, small world.

Every year during my Personal development review (PDR) I told them I wanted to start training nurses on the ward that the course I was updating every year was the Facilitator course and they still sent people down to out-patients. In the end I stopped asking and only updated for personal development.

On one of the in-house study days the Matron had organised she had been talking about documentation and had a real dig at the nurses of our ward, she said our documentation was the worst on the unit, yet we scored the highest in the Audits and as someone who had worked across the board, I knew it wasn't true. In fact, the whole day was crap.

One of the child protection team stated "Women who stay in an abusive relationship and have kids are more bothered about having a man and sex than they are about the safety of their kids"

I was too shocked to say anything. As someone who was once told the only way I would leave my husband was in a box I would say fear is the number one factor in preventing a woman leaving an abusive relationship. I couldn't say anything at the time but inside I was fuming.

Some of the other nurses had also had an issue with the way our ward had been targeted so I decided to speak to our ward manager about it.

I told her How upset I was about what the child protection nurse had said and also about the Matron 'bad mouthing' our ward . I felt better getting it off my chest but it backfired

Instead of backing us up she told the Matron and she came to the ward to speak to me.

She told me I was the only one with the problem and she had spoken to other nurses on the ward and they said it was just me causing trouble.

When she had finished having a go about that she told me that she had lots of complaints about me, she said there was a big complaint in progress by a parent of a child I never met, she told me I had to fill in a statement. I didn't even know who the child was but she didn't listen

" Don't you think it is a coincidence that you were on shift when the complaint was made ? "

" No, because I don't even know the child."

I was in the staff room contemplating leaving when my student came in, she told me she had applied for a job on our ward , I told her I was considering leaving but she said I had to stay because she wanted to work with me as a staff nurse and that is why she had applied to that ward.

When the notes arrived on the ward from the parent who had complained I was asked to write a statement .It turned out the complaint was about the state of the room, the cleaner and the night nurse, I wasn't on that night shift and never met the child or mother. I guess that was my lesson in keeping my opinion to myself in future.

Chris had a leaving party and the whole ward got to go, I asked a few of the girls who had been on the study day if the matron had spoken to them and they said no, she hadn't mentioned it at all. I wasn't surprised to be honest.

I made some fun stuff for Chris's retirement: inspired by Pinterest , I even made a cake shaped like a bedpan, complete with chocolate covered sweet mushrooms as poo and lime jelly as wee, I was really proud of it.

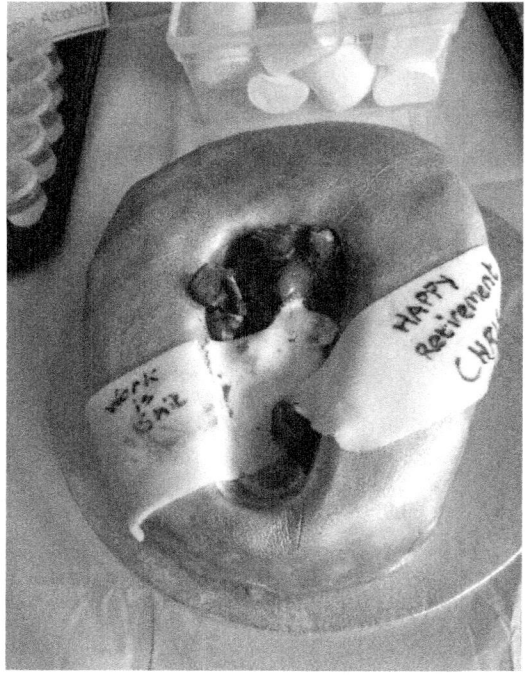

Yes, it is a cake

The whole ward came to the party and brought all kinds of food. We all had a fabulous time, but I was sad to see her leave.

After Chris retired Hannah became more and more disheartened, things were changing and they reduced the amount of clinical nursing she was allowed to do, even though as a clinical support worker she had trained to undertake the role, she felt like a glorified auxiliary . I knew then she wouldn't stick around which was sad because she was excellent at her job.

When Hannah retired, I was the oldest on there, I never realised what a responsibility it was with all the newly qualified and relatively inexperienced staff. I didn't get chance to make her a cake or anything because she retired while I was on my honeymoon and I had been really busy making things for my wedding before that.

I got to be good friends with one of the care assistants, Carron. She was nearer my age and we had a lot in common. Shortly after my return-to-work Carron had an accident at home and fell through her loft floor, she injured her back and pelvis and was in hospital for what seemed like forever. I would often visit her but whenever I asked if she needed anything she told me to do some baking, more often than not she ate the buns while I was there and gave me the box back to refill when I came next time ! I decided to do her extra one time so she could share them with her family or visitors, "not a chance" she said but at least they lasted a bit longer.

One day Carron contacted the ward manager and asked if any of us could go see her on the ward, she was in tears. The ward manager agreed for me and Vicky to go and when we got there the sister on duty told us to go through to the ward.

As I approached the bedside the curtains had been pulled round and there were raised voices, so I called out

"Knock, knock, you aren't having a poo are you"

"No come, in" Carron replied and I could tell she was crying

As I opened the curtain the adult Matron was stood there and she asked us to go and wait outside. We were about to leave but Carron said " No, I want them here , they can listen to what is said"

At that the Matron stormed out and said we had a few minutes and she would be back

Apparently, they had tried to transfer Carron back to another hospital and she had been backwards and forwards that day in the ambulance and was in agony, she was refusing to move but the Matron was insisting.

There wasn't anything we could do but we gave her a little time to calm down and said if she stuck to her guns then maybe they would at least wait until her pain was under control.

As we left the bay the Matron called us over, she said we were very unprofessional and should not be visiting in uniform. I explained we had been asked by the ward manager and also the sister on the ward agreed for us to be here because Carron was so upset.

" "Knock knock , you aren't having a poo ?" Is that how you speak to patients generally ?" she asked in a snide voice "we were having a private conversation and I asked you to wait"

" Well, we work in paediatrics so yes, if a curtain is round, we respect their privacy, that is a normal question to ask ,and we weren't with a patient we were visiting a friend, she wanted us to be there"

" I will be speaking to your matron about your unprofessionalism, there were other patients in the bay and it didn't look good "

" OK" I said

" It wasn't me; it was her" Vicky said

Cheers mate !

I had gone to the cinema with Vicky and Carron , she was not long discharged from hospital and was walking with crutches. When the film finished both Carron and I struggled to get up, Vicky said she should be getting carers allowance cheeky bitch !

Carron started coming to my house once a week and I taught her how to sew, she did an amazing job with a dress she made for her granddaughter and I sent a photo to a sewing magazine, I didn't tell her until it was published, she was buzzing !

I had an afternoon tea party for my birthday and invited a lot of the staff to come, mostly the ones who had visited me when I was off sick or I had seen out of work. I did lots of baking and we started with tea , then moved on to Rum punch for those who weren't driving. It was that successful, it became an annual event. My birthday is in June so most of the time we would have it in the garden, work talk was banned and we had a great time, one year it was raining but it didn't stop me and Vicky from going in the paddling pool.

I noticed there were a few cliques developing as the dynamics changed and it was not the same ward any more. Initially I tried to ignore it but it is hard when the people around you start to be unhappy. I would hear nights out and outings being arranged excluding others deliberately, I had never seen that on there before. I was rarely invited to anything but then I was too old for this kinda shit so didn't care that much. One nurse confided in me she was sad because she knew they were arranging a night out but they had not invited her. When she asked about it, they had even denied it ! I told her at work everyone has to get along, but out of work it is not an obligation to socialise with everyone. You cannot make a friend of someone who doesn't want to be your friend.

Personally, I think sometimes not being invited is a better alternative to being invited and being ostracized. I went to a Christmas Staff party on my last ward and no one spoke to me all night, I thought it was me at first so I tried to join them on the dance floor, they made a circle together and left me on the outside. I have no idea if it was intentional or not, I only know how it made me feel. I ended up going home early in tears. I never went out with the ward team after that.

CHAPTER 13

CANNON FODDER

In 2000 covid hit.

Things really changed for the ward. We were declared a 'clean ward' which meant we only took emergency admissions and all elective surgery was cancelled. No child with suspected covid was to come to the ward,

Some staff were sent to other areas and nurses who were vulnerable came to our ward. I was on medication for colitis so I had been given a letter from my manager saying I had protected status.

But that is not how it worked. All admissions had a covid test on arrival and transferred to the medical unit if positive.

The 'vulnerable' nurses had to carry out these tests and hope they were negative, despite protective equipment it was not a 100% guarantee they were safe, after all we just had basic masks and plastic aprons in the beginning.

Abdominal pain in children is first suspected to be appendicitis so every child with belly ache came to our ward. The main symptom of covid in children is also abdominal pain and a temperature.

When the first test came back positive everyone went into panic mode. The child had been placed in a bay with other children so they all had to be isolated .We would have to contact the medical ward to transfer the children off the ward as soon as possible. This was putting our clean ward in an awkward position.

People were already worried about covid with the hype in the news , many parents were reluctant to bring a child to hospital even when they were sick for fear of contracting this dreaded disease. As nurses we would emphasise the fact, we were a clean ward and they had nothing to worry about but inside we were worried too.

After a few covid positive children had been admitted to the ward it was decided that if they have a temperature, they go to the assessment ward and only come to us after a negative test.

Not all the covid patients had a temperature in the beginning so still a few got through. As a clean ward we probably saw a lot of cases in the beginning. It took months for the management to decide it better that any child should be tested and have a negative test before coming to the ward. Even those with broken bones were tested in A and E and only came if they were negative. Visitors were not allowed and if parents came with a child, they had to test negative too, they were not allowed off the ward for the duration of the child's stay and contracts were drawn up to ensure they knew what was expected of them.

Even as a clean ward we had to take full precautions, we had to wear personal protection equipment (PPE) at all times i.e., masks and aprons and gloves , In the staff room we were only allowed 6 at a time and the tables had markings on where you sat to ensure you were at least 1 metre apart.

It was bleak, in the heat of summer wearing aprons and masks was horrendous, people were irritated and morale was at an all-time low.

The ward itself was dead most of the time, with no elective surgery and more than half the usual Abdo pains being on the medical ward after having blood tests that not only showed negative for covid but also negative for appendicitis.

The staff were encouraged to take annual leave at this time but what was the point ? We couldn't go anywhere or do anything. We didn't know how long it would last and I am sure everyone thought we would be back to normal a lot sooner than we were.

We weren't allowed to discuss the quietness of our ward and having a photo taken in uniform or PPE, sharing anything on social media was a disciplinary offence. I can understand that because there were so many Tik Toks been shared from staff at other hospitals dancing and having a ball while the country was in a state of depression. Regardless of whether or not they were on their breaks it did not look professional for front line staff.

Staff were getting moved to other wards to cover sickness and then returned to the ward putting the other staff at risk. I was even moved a couple of times despite having the exemption letter, apparently that is only there as an advisory. No one was safe, they didn't care who went where, they didn't care about individuals and if anyone declined, they also faced disciplinary action.

One of my colleagues came into work on the night shift and said she was moved to tears by the standing ovation she just witnessed for the NHS and carers. I did not agree at all. In my opinion the clapping on a Thursday night was embarrassing. We certainly didn't deserve it; we had never had it so easy as it was in the beginning.

Some nurses felt proud to be the centre of attention, others knew it was just a front, that once this was over things would be the same, not being appreciated and paid by claps was not as good a thing as the media and government would make you believe.

Those who were on the covid wards had a horrendous time, they weren't heroes they were victims. Some had to move out of their homes to protect their families, sadly some even lost their lives doing what they did best, caring for others. Nurses were the new cannon fodder.

I felt like a tagged criminal, I could go to work and work all day but once home I had to stay there. I couldn't see my friends or family. Even those criminals that are released on tag got to go out during the day.

The sewing lessons with Carron stopped which was annoying, I could work a 12-hour nightshift with her 3 times a week but we weren't allowed to see each other out of work !

I am one of the lucky ones, my husband worked for Waitrose delivering so we always got food and supplies, we didn't need to stockpile things, we knew we could get first chance. We both worked in the frontline so got priority for vaccinations but that didn't help much, we both still contracted it.

Even positive with covid we weren't ill. We redecorated the whole of the first floor in our house and got paid for it ! We have a garden; I could sit out in the garden all day on my days off

But I was still a prisoner.

When covid had got past its peak things were back to normal on the outside but still the PPE was worn on the ward. Staffing levels were continually falling and our ward was constantly used as a bank for other wards and departments.

At Christmas I tried to brighten things up by making stickers to put on our face masks

During lockdown, I joined an online choir, NHS Chorus-19. It was made up from NHS staff past and present from all over the country. The original song was a version of *Come on Eileen* by Dexy's Midnight Runners, reworded as 'Covid 19' and it was such fun to do. We had online coaching

from the lovely Anna Lapwood and although I wasn't very good, I did feel like I had an outlet and looked forward to the online class every week. My voice improved with all the practice and vocal exercises but I am not quite ready to release my own music album ha ha.

Carron joined the choir too and although we could not be together to do the singing, we both enjoyed the outlet. We made recordings and sent them in, the voices were then synched and released on YouTube for us to watch or the sound file sent for us to listen to. We never did get to hear the covid 19 one though so don't know what happened to it, maybe it was too close for comfort .

The first recording of over the rainbow actually brought tears to my eyes.

We were given the opportunity to sing with Russell Watson at Audley End for the last night at the Heritage Proms, a once in a lifetime opportunity. It would mean taking annual leave to give me the two weekends I needed for the rehearsals and the performance. I was told the annual leave for that week was already full so unless I could get someone to swap, I wouldn't be able to go.

Carron was told she couldn't have the time off either but she only worked at the weekends so she understood, she didn't have any annual leave left to take anyway.

I wasn't happy, the ward was not the same. , you never knew when going to work if you would be moved. Even if you didn't get moved you were left behind short staffed so it was a no-win situation. The decisions were made by people much higher up and it wasn't optional. They looked at numbers not acuity

I was struggling increasingly with knee pain but with limited doctors' appointments it was difficult to get anything done about it. I just kept taking the painkillers and hoping for the best.

The shift patterns had changed too, half an hour was stolen from the night shift so instead of a 12 hour shift it was an 11 ½ hour shift , that meant on the weeks I worked a night shift I owed them 30 minutes a shift. I was getting more and more 'extra' shifts to make up for the shortfall in hours which didn't seem to add up with my calendar but it was fruitless arguing about it. My main problem was working two long days together and with the extra shift it often meant that I would have two together . The pain was horrendous without a day to rest in-between.

I asked about changing my hours to two nights or long days and a short shift to make it up to my 30 hours. This wasn't very practical on the ward as it would mean someone else doing the half a shift.

I started working in outpatients for my short shift and for a while it was great. I always worked the Friday there and then the two weekend nights, or sometimes two shifts in the week.

My shifts started creeping together and I found it just as hard in outpatients as I was on my feet all day, the job down there was only temporary for 6 months anyway so in May I moved back up to the ward .

I said I may as well go back to three-night shifts one week and two long days the next, one week I had 4-day shifts and when I queried it, I was told it was my 3-day week and hours I owed them, I had no idea how I had accrued 12 hours in such a short time back but it was from 'before' they said.

I asked why I couldn't get my extra shift on the 2-day week and I was told " You work for us , not the other way around " Wow ! How to make your staff feel valued !

That was my turning point. I went home and I was so angry, I discussed it with Nigel and felt It was time I got out before I say something I regret.

The next day I gave in my notice.

I really wanted to go to the choir event too so this would kill two birds with one stone, If I retired by the middle of August, I would be free to go down to Cambridge in time for the rehearsals. Nigel booked time off too and we booked our caravan in on a site nearby.

The ward manager tried to tell me I couldn't give it in then, it had to be on the first of a month, so that meant I would give it in on the first of June, she said I would have to work until the end of August anyway. Yeah right !

When I left the office, I went into the linen room with my mobile phone and called HR straight away ,they told me this was not true and in fact as a staff nurse, I need only give 6 weeks' notice but 3 months is optimal so they can get my pension ready.

I went back to give my letter to the ward manager and I told her HR said I could give my notice any day and count the time from that day, it did not have to be the beginning of the month at all. She tried to say things had changed recently so my information was probably outdated and she was right, I told her I only phoned them ten minutes before so that was not true, she left the office and said she would see me after lunch about it.

At lunchtime the ward sister told me the ward manager was going home sick and she wasn't allowed to take my resignation, I demanded to see the matron but at that moment the manager came into the staff room. I gave her the letter and told the sister to witness it

"File it, do what you want with it but today is the day you received it and I have a witness" I said

Things became quite tense on the ward but I was leaving so I didn't care until one night shift and they told me I had to go to the medical ward. They knew how anxious I got going on that ward but they didn't care, it had come from above and I had no choice.

I collected my things and walked off the ward. When I got to the tower block the lift was broken. I started to walk up the stairs but after three flights I was in agony, I started to hyperventilate, I felt dizzy and honestly thought I would pass out. I called the ward and told them I would have to take it slow so could they inform the medical ward.

There was nowhere to sit and I couldn't stop crying. One of the girls from the ward called to tell me to take it slow she had informed the ward. I was on the 8th floor by then , I couldn't speak, she realised I was distressed and spoke to the nurse in charge, she told me to go back and one of them would go instead. I told her if I went back down the stairs I was going home.

When I made it to the ward it wasn't so bad, the nurses on duty were ones I didn't know and were pretty understanding. They said they weren't that busy anyway so not to worry

THEY WERE NOT THAT BUSY !

The ward I left WAS busy and I left them understaffed, but hey they knew how I felt about the other ward and sat there so why should I care.

I was given two patients, an anorexic who needed night meds and then went to sleep and a baby who was on phototherapy. As I walked towards the baby the doctor approached and said that the baby could come off phototherapy and probably be going home the next day so just for basic observations overnight. Mum was resident so she did all his basic cares.

After a few hours once the nurses on there were sorted, they told me I could go back if I wanted. So, at 12 midnight I went back to my own ward, they had settled all the children so as I had no patients, I covered breaks.

The next day I went to my doctors and told him about my severe knee pain. I told him my shifts had made it impossible for me to continue my job and I had given in my notice, he asked how long I had left and gave me a sick note to cover that period, I never went back

In the same week I contacted the NMC and cancelled my registration

I didn't want to be a nurse any more, I didn't want to be tempted back. I was done !

I received a thankyou from the trust after I left for my support through Covid, I even got a commemorative coin, I suppose that it a little like a war medal

HULL UNIVERSITY TEACHING HOSPITALS NHS TRUST

WE THANK YOU · WE THINK OF THEM

NHS · COVID-19 PANDEMIC · 2020-21

ON JANUARY 29TH, 2020, OUR STAFF TREATED THE FIRST CONFIRMED CASES OF COVID-19 IN THE UK. IN THE YEAR THAT FOLLOWED, 12,000 OF OUR PEOPLE SUPPORTED 38,000 OTHERS WHO CONTRACTED THE DISEASE. FOR SOME, SADLY IT WASN'T ENOUGH. THEY WILL BE DEARLY MISSED BY THEIR FAMILIES AND ALWAYS REMEMBERED BY US.

My reward for 40 years of nursing was in the form of gift vouchers, high street gift vouchers, £5 for every year of service. Now don't get me wrong, this is a nice gesture but most of the high street shops listed had closed down and many that hadn't been still closed post covid. I don't really wear jewellery and at my age I have started storing ornaments in the loft due to lack of space so I had no clue of what to do with them.

I tried to use them online but apparently the paper vouchers can only be used in store. In the end I bought some paint and a lampshade from Wilkos to redecorate my bedroom, and spent the rest in Iceland buying party food for Christmas.

Thanks NHS , it's been a blast !

We had an amazing time in Cambridge, the rehearsals were surreal. How could we sound so good when none of us had ever met before , never mind sang together. This wasn't digitally enhanced singing; it was the real thing and I felt so proud to be part of it.

Standing on that stage singing to thousands of people was a great achievement and I will never forget it. I am so glad I didn't miss it.

We sang together again in October 2021 at the Royal festival hall in London with the Bach choir and Royal Philharmonic orchestra. The choir seemed to have dried up now as people got back to their normal life but I feel honoured to have taken part.

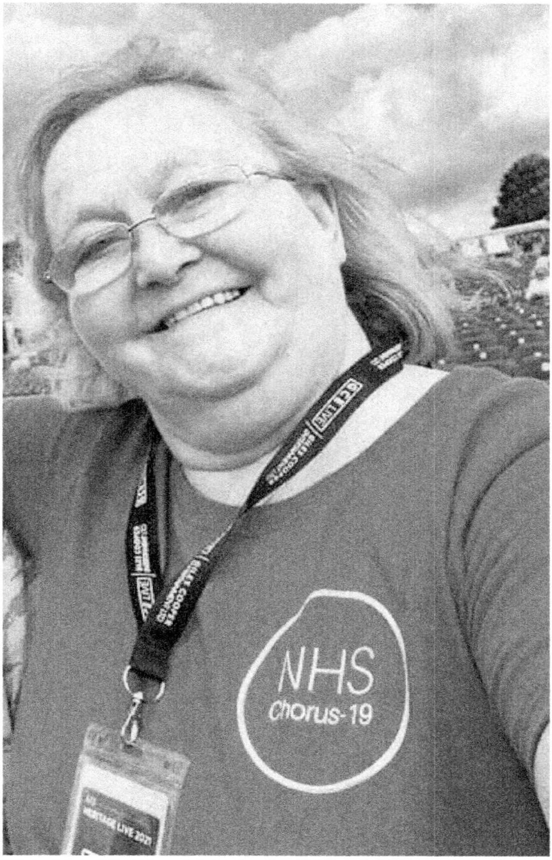
NHS
Chorus-19

Singing on the stage at Audley End

About The Author:

Carol Scrimshaw is the youngest of six children and has 3 grown up children from her first marriage. Originally from Bradford, she has Now remarried and settled in Kingston upon Hull.

Carol has a 40-year nursing career and is a qualified paediatric nurse.

Now retired from nursing she is focused on her crafting business and writing her memoirs.

My First book:
**Fact or Fiction:
You Couldn't Make This Shit Up**
is also available on Amazon

Printed in Great Britain
by Amazon